• • •

THE
ENDURING FAITH
AND
TIMELESS TRUTHS
OF
FULTON SHEEN

• • •

Mark J. Zia, S.T.D.

servant
AN IMPRINT OF
FRANCISCAN MEDIA
Cincinnati, Ohio

RESCRIPT

In accord with the *Code of Canon Law*, I hereby grant my permission to publish *The Enduring Faith and Timeless Teachings of Fulton Sheen*, by Mark J. Zia, S.T.D.

Most Reverend Joseph F. Naumann
Archbishop of Kansas City in Kansas
Kansas City
January 28, 2015

The permission to publish is a declaration that a book or pamphlet is considered to be free from doctrinal or moral error. It is not implied that those who have granted the permission to publish agree with the contents, opinions or statements expressed.

Scripture passages have been taken from the *Revised Standard Version*, Catholic edition. Copyright 1946, 1952, 1971 by the Division of Christian Education of the National Council of Churches of Christ in the USA. Used by permission. All rights reserved. Quotes are taken from the English translation of the *Catechism of the Catholic Church* for the United States of America (indicated as CCC), 2nd ed. Copyright 1997 by United States Catholic Conference—Libreria Editrice Vaticana.

Cover design by Candle Light Studio
Cover image © Copyright Bettmann I Corbis I AP Images
Book Design by Mark Sullivan

LIBRARY OF CONGRESS CATALOGING-IN-PUBLICATION DATA
Zia, Mark J.
The enduring faith and timeless teachings of Fulton Sheen / Mark J. Zia, S.T.D.
pages cm
Includes bibliographical references.
ISBN 978-1-61636-943-9 (alk. paper)
1. Sheen, Fulton J. (Fulton John), 1895-1979. 2. Catholic Church—Doctrines. I. Title.
BX4705.S612Z53 2015
282.092—dc23
2015011886

ISBN 978-1-61636-943-9

Published by Servant Books,
an imprint of Franciscan Media
28 W. Liberty St.
Cincinnati, OH 45202
www.FranciscanMedia.org

Printed in the United States of America.
Printed on acid-free paper.
15 16 17 18 19 5 4 3 2

To my oldest son, Luca,
who shares his May 8 birthday
with Archbishop Fulton J. Sheen,

~

and to my pastor,
Fr. Gerard Senecal, O.S.B. (1929–2015),
who had the heart of Sheen.

CONTENTS

I am very grateful to Mark J. Zia for asking me to write a foreword for his book *The Enduring Faith of Fulton Sheen.* It presents a very comprehensive view of the theology of Archbishop Fulton J. Sheen. This book offers a great service for the Catholic Church at a time when many of the faithful are looking for clear, easy-to-understand, and solidly Catholic material on the teachings of the Church.

Archbishop Sheen was particularly qualified to offer such teachings. A brief look at his academic achievements as well as his teaching career will make this quite evident. His theological formation actually began in his childhood family life because his home truly possessed a Catholic spirit. His parents were devout Catholics. There was prayer in the family, particularly the daily family rosary. He went to Catholic grammar school and high school. He attended St. Viator College in Bourbonnais, Illinois, where he laid the groundwork for his future teaching, preaching, and writing by joining the school's debate team and newspaper staff. In preparation for becoming a priest, he studied theology at St. Paul's Seminary in Saint Paul, Minnesota, and was ordained a priest in St. Mary's Cathedral in Peoria, Illinois, on September 20, 1919.

After ordination, his bishop sent him to the Catholic University of America in Washington, D.C., to obtain a doctorate in sacred theology. After two years there, he transferred to the Catholic

University of Louvain in Belgium to study the theology of St. Thomas in greater depth. In 1923, he obtained a doctorate at Louvain. He did so well that he was invited to study there for a degree called the "agrégé," a kind of super-doctorate that would allow him to teach in the various Catholic universities in Europe. He graduated with outstanding distinction. There is evidence that he later earned a second doctorate in theology at the Angelicum in Rome.

There was a very interesting anecdote in connection with the celebration of his winning the agrégé that tells us something of his intellectual ability. A special dinner was held in honor of anyone who won the agrégé degree. Attendees could tell how well the individual did in the grueling daylong exams by what was served as a drink at the special dinner. If the individual just passed, water was served. If he did a little better, beer was provided. If he did even better, servers brought out wine. And if the individual did extremely well, the attendees celebrated with champagne. It is said that there were buckets and buckets of champagne on the table for the meal to celebrate Fr. Fulton Sheen's winning the agrégé! He was the first American ever to win this prestigious degree. During his time in Europe, he also studied at the Sorbonne in Paris and taught dogmatic theology at St. Edmund's College in Ware, England. He also won the distinguished Cardinal Mercier Prize for International Philosophy in 1923.

His bishop called him back to the United States. After spending eight months in a poor, inner-city parish in Peoria, where he visited the homes of every parishioner and got many of them to come back to church, his bishop sent him to teach at the Catholic University of America. After teaching dogmatic theology for a short time, he moved to the Department of Philosophy, where he taught philosophy and religion for twenty-four years, from 1926 to 1950. His classes were extremely popular, and his classroom was often filled by as many non-enrolled participants as regular students. While teaching at Catholic University, Sheen began his work as a radio evangelist. He would often travel to New York City, where he would preach at a church in midtown Manhattan to an overflowing crowd. At the same time, his talks were broadcast over local radio in New York City. In 1930, the bishops of the United States chose him to be the voice of *The Catholic Hour* broadcast, which reached an estimated listening audience of four to six million people every Sunday afternoon. These broadcasts had solidly Catholic content. His fame and influence as an author, preacher, and teacher of the faith grew immensely.

His greatest fame, however, would come as a televangelist, beginning in 1951 with his very popular TV program, *Life Is Worth Living*. That fall one of the major networks wanted to present a program of religious content--in that era, the networks had an obligation to do so for about half an hour each week. Now a bishop, Sheen was chosen to present the program. He was put opposite Milton Berle, who at the time was known as "Mr. Television." There was a feeling that no one could compete with Berle. Amazingly, however, within six months, more people were watching Bishop Fulton J. Sheen on Tuesday nights from 7:00 to 7:30 p.m. than were watching Milton Berle. Sheen's viewing audience grew to approximately twenty-five to thirty million people. He won an Emmy in 1952 for "the most outstanding personality on television," beating out Lucille Ball, Edward R. Morrow, and others.

What made him so popular with a general audience of more non-Catholics than Catholics? First, he was clear and simple in presenting his message. He brought his message down to a level an average person had no problem understanding. Of the three main religious groups in the United States at the time—namely Catholics, Protestants, and Jewish people—it was estimated that the highest percentage of his audience was Jewish, the second highest was Protestant, and the third was Catholic.

Second, Sheen used a lot of humor to express his teachings. He took examples from everyday life and did not hesitate to make himself the subject of his own jokes. When he received his Emmy at the award ceremony, he said, "I want to thank my writers, Matthew, Mark, Luke, and John." His smile as well as his riveting eyes—which seemed to penetrate right into people's hearts and souls—attracted many to him.

Third, he spoke with conviction. He showed that he believed what he was saying. He was a great believer in truth and always proclaimed it as best he could. He used to say, "The truth is the truth even if nobody believes it. And error is error even if everybody believes it." People trusted him because of his allegiance to truth. He did not try to be politically correct or sway the crowds. He knew that he had an obligation to lead people to a truth that would make them free (see John 8:32) from confusion, distortion, and falsehood. He had a responsibility to help people grow. One of his most famous sayings was reportedly, "If you want people to remain the way they are, just tell them what they *want* to hear. And if you want people to change for the better, tell them what they *need* to hear."

Mark Zia, throughout his book *The Enduring Faith of Fulton Sheen*, quotes from many of the archbishop's sixty-five books.

Venerable Servant of God Fulton Sheen could truly be called a model for the New Evangelization that Pope St. John Paul II, Pope Benedict XVI, and Pope Francis call us to embrace. Fulton Sheen used the main forms of media in his day—namely television, radio, and the written word—to spread the truth of the Gospel as a light for the salvation and sanctification of souls as well as a love that would bring unity and peace to all mankind. In my work as the vice postulator for the cause of Archbishop Fulton J. Sheen, I often hope in my heart that if he is canonized, God willing, he would be declared a Doctor of the Church and possibly a patron saint for the New Evangelization. Only God can bring this about, if he so wills.

Archbishop Sheen used to say that radio evangelization was like the Old Testament: You only hear the Word but see nothing. He compared television evangelization to the New Testament: You not only can hear but see. Through his preaching, teaching, and writing, it is estimated that Bishop Sheen converted approximately forty-two thousand to the faith, in addition to many personal conversions. I am grateful that Mark Zia has presented many of the teachings of Fulton Sheen in a new format that will enrich the lives of all those who are seeking truth and trying to understand the challenging times we live in.

One of the great graces of my life was that on March 16, 1967, Bishop Fulton Sheen, then bishop of Rochester, New York, ordained me a priest. Priesthood is such a great grace. Sheen loved being a priest, and he conveyed some of that love to me. He said in the homily at my Ordination Mass: "The emotional thrill of the First Mass will leave, but not the love of being a priest—that grows as the years go on!" How right he was!

I often reflect on his words, both in his talks and in his writings. One catches some of the power of the Holy Spirit that seems to come through him both in his spoken and written word. I joined the Archbishop Fulton Sheen Foundation to promote his cause for canonization because I did not want to see his voice go silent in the Church. He has too much to offer us!

May God bless this work of Mark Zia, *The Enduring Faith of Fulton Sheen*, and use it as an instrument to instruct and inspire many people in our time. And may Our Lady, to whom Sheen was so dedicated, help all of us through his example to come closer to God. As he expressed in the words he chose as his episcopal motto on his coat of arms: "Grant that I may come to Thee through Mary."

—Fr. Andrew Apostoli, C.F.R.
Vice-postulator for the cause
for canonization of Archbishop
Fulton J. Sheen
Bronx, New York

America needs a saint, an American saint...a saint who would be a priest, and preferably a bishop, to prove that sanctity in a nation must begin with the bishops.[1]
—Fulton Sheen, *Missions and the World Crisis*

It may be said that in every age, God raises up saints who best exemplify the virtues needed in order to combat the particular evils of the time and place. Archbishop Fulton J. Sheen was one such man. Yet his example is just as relevant for us in the twenty-first century as for those of the twentieth century in which he lived and ministered.

There are five aspects of Sheen that are especially relevant to us today and that make his life attractive to us: He was a contemporary American; he exhibited a wonderful sense of humor; he possessed great wisdom; he was a Catholic bishop; and his life was one of holiness.

First, Sheen was a contemporary American. It can sometimes be difficult for us to relate to holy men and women of other historical periods and other nations. The fact that Sheen was "homegrown" and flourished in the twentieth century makes his witness more credible in our eyes.

Second, Sheen's sense of humor was legendary. Too often we get the impression that holiness and virtue are incompatible with humor and wit, but Sheen refreshingly reminds us that the joy that animates our hearts with the love of Christ overflows into other areas of our lives. His appreciation of a good laugh, especially at his own expense, made him a person whom others wanted to be around. This held true even when his message was countercultural or otherwise difficult for sinful humanity to accept.

Third, Sheen was exceedingly wise. Whereas knowledge pertains to how well one can assimilate and understand facts and concepts, wisdom is a special gift of God whereby one can discern God's plan and take the right course of action in pursuing that plan. We have many smart people but far fewer truly wise persons. Sheen demonstrates the true wisdom that can be found only in Christ and in the pursuit of his will.

Fourth, Sheen was a Catholic bishop. Bishops are successors of the apostles who have the threefold duty of teaching, governing, and sanctifying the Church. Although all Christians are called to participate in the Church's mission to preach the Gospel to every nation, there is something especially fitting about a bishop being recognized as preeminent in this role.

Finally, Sheen's cooperation with God's grace—as evidenced through his deep spiritual life, daily Holy Hours, and lived holiness—was crucial to the success of his ministry. Never overly proud of his accomplishments or arrogant toward those less learned than he, Sheen constantly credited God for everything good in his life. Sheen was a living reminder that all of us are called to heroic virtue and a life of holiness in service to others.

In this book, I will revisit some of Archbishop Sheen's teachings on the faith and invite you to consider their application to your life. Through this modest effort to understand better the big picture of the enduring Catholic faith through the insights of this holy man, I pray that we may all come to a greater appreciation of our faith and develop a fervent desire to proclaim it to others in a spirit of charity and joy.

CHAPTER ONE

Fulton J. Sheen: Teacher of the Faith

It is always a revelation of disastrous failure when people are impressed more with what a man knows than with what a man is, or more with the college from which he was graduated than with his virtue. [1]

—Fulton Sheen, *For God and Country*

Fulton Sheen, eight years old, was serving Mass at the cathedral for Bishop John Lancaster Spalding, the first bishop of the diocese of Peoria. Spalding had attended the Catholic University of Louvain in Belgium and was considered "the leading Catholic educator in the period between the Civil War and the World War."[2] Young Fulton accidently dropped one of the cruets on the marble floor of the sanctuary. The cruet smashed into countless pieces with a loud crash, and some seventy years later Sheen still recounted that "there is no atomic explosion that can equal in intensity of decibels the noise and explosive force of a wine cruet falling on the marble floor of a cathedral in the presence of a bishop."[3]

After Mass, the kind bishop addressed the young Fulton: "Go home and tell your mother that I said when you get big you are to go to Louvain, and someday you will be just as I am."[4]

Perhaps a scolding or a public humiliation would have discouraged the boy enough to ignore his priestly vocation. In pointing out that a vocation is a far more important concern than a little accident, the bishop showed Sheen that even the most unexpected circumstances can be a means of evangelization.

In his adult life, Sheen was extremely successful in presenting the Gospel message—on radio and television and through his thirty years as a university professor. Although educational technology has advanced light years beyond his chalkboard presentations, the content and philosophical underpinnings of his preaching and teaching retain their value. His wisdom and insight can be of great benefit to clergy and laity of our era. For the bishop's comment about his own era is perhaps even truer of our time: "Never before in history has there been so much thinking and so little coming to the knowledge of truth, so many schools and so little scholarship, so many wise men and so little wisdom, so much talking about religion and so little prayer."[5]

Some of the essential attributes of an effective teacher can be gleaned by examining Sheen's own pedagogy. His was zeal for truth, a good sense of humor, a keen awareness of his own limitations, preparedness to engage, and authenticity. By exploring some of his pedagogical underpinnings in this first chapter, we will be better prepared to read the remaining chapters in the spirit of Sheen's own style and outlook.

THE SPLENDOR OF TRUTH

A cornerstone of education is the systematic pursuit and acquisition of truth. Sadly, many educational institutions today, from grade school through university, focus not on truth but on utility, practicality, and economic success. Sheen comments, "If there is any great characteristic of our age, it is want of zeal for truth....

There is no fire in our hearts, but only dying embers."[6]

Sometimes products of this defective method of education themselves, parents may tell their children, "No, you really don't want to major in art. You cannot do anything worthwhile with an art degree." Or, "You should major in business, since then you can have a well-paying and practical career." Even "good Catholic parents" might ask a young man or woman, "Why would you ever want to enter religious life? What bragging rights could we possibly have?"

The liberal arts are thrown out the window in favor of professional programs that promise high starting salaries and prestige after graduation. This is not to say that there is anything wrong with pursuing a professional degree. Sheen would be among the first to value such education, as long as students are also educated in the liberal arts and the pursuit of truth for its own sake. The things to avoid are the drive for financial gain and the need for prestigious career placement.

As for the liberal arts curriculum, Sheen also warns of the dangers when students take a hodgepodge assortment of unrelated classes simply to earn enough credits to graduate:

> Students are not getting the education they ought to receive; they get only a congeries of unrelated, disconnected, and disjointed subjects, which they and no one else can put together. An encyclopedia is not educated, despite its bursting with knowledge, because it lacks the power to coordinate one subject with another. A truly educated man, on the contrary, sees a relationship between subjects.... Any system of electives which ignores the unity of knowledge and the over-all purpose of life confuses the student rather than perfects him in truth.[7]

The situation is complicated even more by the fact that many educational institutions today are infected with secularism and utilitarianism—to the point that Sheen asks, "Would it not be well to establish universities in this country dedicated to the purpose not of learning but of unlearning?"[8] He is drawing attention to the fact that in many instances, the type of education a student receives is riddled with falsehoods and half-truths, particularly concerning a proper understanding of the human person: his origins, values, and destiny. "We might just as well put it bluntly, and say that what we call modern is only an old error with a new label. The modern view of man is wrong—completely and absolutely wrong, and if we go on following it we will end in blind alleys, frustrated hopes and unhappy existences."[9]

Thus the authentic teacher may need to divest students of intellectual nonsense they have received before giving them the truth about themselves and the world around them. The focus of education must be on truth, not on political correctness and trendy theories. Above all, students need a proper introduction to Christian anthropology in order to understand and take control of their futures. For education is ultimately about growing in virtue and becoming saints of the kingdom of heaven. Sheen puts it this way:

> What has complicated and intensified parental irresponsibility is the fact that most schools today assume that education consists only of the *imparting of knowledge*. This is an egregious error, because knowledge is only a part of education, and this means the will must be trained as well as the intellect. More important than knowledge is the formation of character, the right ordering of conscience, and the formation of personality.[10]

GOOD FOR A LAUGH

A truly effective preacher or educator will not be afraid to employ humor at appropriate times. Sheen certainly demonstrated its capacity to perk up an audience. He wrote, "Whether there be only five senses or fifty-seven senses, one of the most precious of them all is the one the modern world is rapidly losing, namely, the sense of humor."[11]

Sheen's humor, even when dealing with serious topics, was part of his charm, endearing him to many people. He recalls one example in his autobiography:

> This reminds me of a lecture I was giving to a group of university students in Minnesota. In the question period that followed, one asked me how Jonah was in the belly of the whale for three days. I answered: "I have not the vaguest idea, but when I get to Heaven, I will ask Jonah." He shouted back: "Suppose Jonah isn't there." I said: "Then you ask him."[12]

Another humorous exchange was at Sheen's expense:

> I gave many lectures in Philadelphia and each year for a number of years, one was given at the Town Hall. One evening I lost my way and asked a few boys for directions. They told me where it was and then they asked: "What are you going to do there?" I said: "I'm going to give a lecture." "On what?" they asked. I did not tell them the title of the lecture but simplified it by saying: "Boys, I'm going to talk on Heaven and how to get there. Would you like to come and find out?" They said: "You don't even know the way to the Town Hall."[13]

Many other episodes of humor took Sheen quite by surprise. For example:

> I finished a triduum in one parish. The church was crowded and we invited the young children to sit in the sanctuary. There were probably fifty or sixty of them under the age of ten. I went into the church about an hour before the sermon and knelt down on a prie-dieu to meditate. Afterward the sheriff of the town told me that his little daughter was among those who were in the sanctuary that night. She asked her father, "Why did the bishop kneel there looking straight at the altar so long?" "He was probably talking to God." The little girl said: "I thought he was God."[14]

Sheen recalled an instance that put him on the receiving end of someone's impatience. Although the event may have been embarrassing, he did not hesitate to share it for its humor:

> One Sunday, preaching in a parish church in Ohio, a mother in the front seat got up with a crying child and quickly made her exit down the middle aisle. I stopped the sermon and said: "Madam, do not worry, the child is not disturbing me." She said: "No, but you're disturbing the child."[15]

HUMILITY AND PREPAREDNESS

Another essential quality of an effective teacher is humility. This is perhaps not too common in an age that exalts the ego above everything else. It can be very tempting for a professor in the front of a classroom to exhibit a condescending smugness, a distinguished superiority to his students.

Sheen takes the vice of pride very seriously: "All our other sins can be from ourselves; for example, avarice, lust, anger, gluttony. But pride comes direct from hell. By that sin fell the angels. It destroys the very possibility of conversion."[16]

In the classroom, Sheen observes, this vice can be found in two expressions, which he refers to as "pride of omniscience" and "pride of nescience." He explains, "The pride of omniscience tries to convince your neighbour you know everything; the new pride of nescience tries to convince your neighbour that he knows nothing."[17]

To avoid these temptations, teachers need to remember that not even they have all the answers. Perhaps they would find it helpful to call to mind an example recounted by Sheen: "Michelangelo, who lived to be almost ninety, often used to repeat his motto as he chiseled marble that almost spoke: 'I still learn.'"[18]

Another indispensable characteristic of an effective educator is preparedness. Sheen wryly commented, "I have found, after thirty years in universities, that the more books the professor brings into class, the less prepared he is."[19]

The tendency to walk unprepared into a classroom is minimal in primary and secondary schools, where lesson plans must generally be submitted beforehand. University professors have no such requirement. When they go into a classroom in a haphazard manner, they send a message to the students that what they are going to discuss in that class period is not important enough to prepare beforehand.

Compare this "method" to Sheen's own. He tells us that he spent at least six hours preparing for every one hour of class lecture.[20] Even more impressive is the fact that he spent thirty hours preparing for each of his television appearances.[21] And Sheen prepared all of his sermons in the presence of the Blessed Sacrament.[22]

ENGAGEMENT AND AUTHENTICITY

Another necessary quality of an effective educator is engagement with one's students and with the subject matter at hand. Unfortunately, "some professors are merely textbooks wired for sound. Teaching is too often reduced to the communication of the notes on the professor's yellow pages to the white pages of a student's notebook, without passing through the minds of either."[23] This type of knowledge can be acquired just as well at home online or through a book.

Rather, professors need to walk their students through the reasoning process and help them understand the relevance of the subject matter for both practical and theoretical judgments. The ultimate aim is to help students seek and acquire truth and virtue. Such engagement encourages professors to stay current with research in their fields, mindful of the fact that "a teacher who himself does not learn is no teacher."[24]

Sheen strongly believed that "there is nothing that so much destroys the intellectual growth of the teacher as the keeping of notes and the repetition of the same course the following year."[25] A student-centered classroom focused on academic engagement is less likely to fall into this type of rut. Sheen was not a supporter of the tenure system, since professors who obtain tenure have little incentive to retain their engagement with their students and with their academic discipline. They can too easily choose to "get by" with their teaching.

Sheen makes his point by a comparison with football coaches: "Why is it that we teachers have tenure and football coaches do not? There can be mediocrity in the classroom. A football coach who does not produce a winning team is forced to leave. Old generals may fade away—but poor teachers are just handed on."[26]

Finally, Sheen demonstrates the importance of authenticity in the classroom. He always maintained a Christ-centered focus in all of his teaching, not because he was a bishop but simply because he was Catholic. He used to say, "If you know Christ, it does not matter if you know nothing else; but if you know not Christ, it is as nothing to know everything else."[27]

These words reinforce his view of education: namely, that its ultimate purpose is to lead us to heaven, a theme we will probe in the next chapter of this book. Authenticity demands that the truths learned about the moral life be actually carried out in our everyday dealings with one another rather than be confined to the intellectual domain. In real life, faith and practice are integrated, and they generally stand or fall together.

It is interesting to note that many of those who claim to reject the Catholic Church on intellectual grounds actually reject it on moral issues, as Sheen points out:

> Minds no longer object to the Church because of the way they *think*, but because of the way they *live*. They no longer have difficulty with the Creed, but with her Commandments; they remain outside her saving waters, not because they cannot accept the doctrine of the Three Persons in One God, but because they cannot accept the moral of two persons in one flesh; not because Infallibility is too complex, but because the veto on Birth Control is too hard; not because the Eucharist is too sublime, but

because Penance is too exacting. Briefly, the heresy of our day is not the heresy of thought; it is the heresy of action.[28]

Sheen helps us remember that education is not only about discovering truth; it is about putting that truth into action at the service of oneself and one's neighbor. Sheen writes, "All of the tragedies of Catholicism arise from the failure of individual Catholics to rise to their opportunities and to permeate their social and intellectual environment with their faith."[29] May we never place barriers between our learning and our believing but rather allow faith and reason to uphold and sustain one another.

THE FIRST TEACHERS

Discussion about Sheen's educational philosophy would be incomplete without pointing out the primacy of the family in the education of children. Sheen calls to mind a story told of Napoleon: "Napoleon was once asked, 'When does the education of a child begin?' and his answer was: 'Twenty years before its birth, in the education of its mother.'"[30]

Sheen wrote that "the teacher only *supplements*, but never *supplants* either the right or duty of parents."[31] Twenty years later, the Second Vatican Council articulated this same teaching:

> Parents are the ones who must create a family atmosphere animated by love and respect for God and man, in which the well-rounded personal and social education of children is fostered. Hence the family is the first school of the social virtues that every society needs.... Here, too, [children] find their first experience of a wholesome human society and of the Church. Finally, it is through the family that they are gradually led to a companionship with their fellowmen and with the people of God....[32]

Pope St. John Paul II also firmly defended this teaching:

> The right and duty of parents to give education is essen-
> tial, since it is connected with the transmission of human
> life; it is original and primary with regard to the educa-
> tional role of others, on account of the uniqueness of the
> loving relationship between parents and children; and it is
> irreplaceable and inalienable, and therefore incapable of
> being entirely delegated to others or usurped by others.[33]

While it is true that parents will be the first teachers of their children with respect to what we consider academic subjects, even
greater is their role as the first teachers of virtue. Parents are called
to manifest their love for their children by being living examples
of virtue and holiness. John Paul II advised:

> It cannot be forgotten that the most basic element, so
> basic that it qualifies the educational role of parents, is
> parental love, which finds fulfillment in the task of educa-
> tion as it completes and perfects its service of life: as well
> as being a source, the parents' love is also the animating
> principle and therefore the norm inspiring and guiding all
> concrete educational activity, enriching it with the values
> of kindness, constancy, goodness, service, disinterested-
> ness and self-sacrifice that are the most precious fruit of
> love.[34]

For the optimum success and happiness of the child, this modeling
is to be done by a father and a mother who are united in the bonds
of sacred matrimony, as taught by the Second Vatican Council:

The family is a kind of school of deeper humanity. But if it is to achieve the full flowering of its life and mission, it needs the kindly communion of minds and the joint deliberation of spouses, as well as the painstaking cooperation of parents in the education of their children. The active presence of the father is highly beneficial to their formation. The children, especially the younger among them, need the care of their mother at home. This domestic role of hers must be safely preserved, though the legitimate social progress of women should not be underrated on that account.[35]

THE TRUTH ABOUT TOLERANCE

Today we see a growing number of politicians endorsing government regulations to keep abortion legal, widely distribute contraception, sanction gay marriage, allow homosexual couples to adopt children, and give transgendered people legal recognition. Our educational system has begun to teach these aberrations to the youngest of children. There is an attempt to convince them that these are all normal and healthy choices. Parents have to reclaim the right to teach their children sound morals, age-appropriate sexual education, and the integration of all forms of knowledge with our quest for holiness. Perhaps it may be said more today than decades ago, "being a true Christian...does not require an education. *It is an education!*"[36]

What about tolerance concerning these controversial topics? Sheen writes, "Tolerance applies only to persons, but never to truth. Intolerance applies only to truth, but never to persons."[37] He means that we are called to love individuals, even those who are attempting to destroy the moral fabric of our society, but to be strongly intolerant of all falsehood.

America, it is commonly said, is suffering from intolerance. While there is much want of charity to our fellow-citizens, I believe it is truer to say that America is not suffering so much from intolerance as it is suffering from a false kind of tolerance: the tolerance of right and wrong; truth and error; virtue and vice; Christ and chaos.[38]

Is intolerance a Christian option? Sheen responds in the affirmative:

He [Christ] was tolerant about where He slept and what He ate; He was tolerant about shortcomings of His fish-smelling apostles; He was tolerant of those who nailed Him to the Cross, but He was absolutely intolerant about His claim to be Divine.... The world may charge the Church with intolerance, and the world is right. The Church is intolerant—intolerant about Truth, intolerant about principles, intolerant about Divinity, just as Our Blessed Lord was intolerant about His Divinity.[39]

In summary, Sheen was a wonderful preacher and teacher who drew record numbers to his engagements. By taking note of the qualities of this dynamic teacher and making them our own, we also can be effective witnesses to the enduring truths of our rich Catholic faith. We have entered the era of evangelization by the laity, so rather than await another Fulton Sheen, let us seek to embody his virtues and continue to bring the Gospel to the ends of the earth. Sheen would want it, our Church wants it, and the Holy Father wants it.

I invite you to stay with me as we systematically explore Sheen's teachings on essential Catholic doctrines. My hope is that you can become better equipped to carry on the wonderful task of evangelization!

Points to Ponder

- Which of Sheen's pedagogical skills or methods do you find most helpful? How can you incorporate these into your life?
- In what practical ways can you bring Sheen's wisdom into your family, your parish, your classroom, or your workplace?
- If Sheen were alive today and still teaching, how do you think the media would react to him?

CHAPTER TWO

The Universal Call to Holiness

A civilization is not superior because it has more bath-
tubs and electric switches, deeper tunnels and taller build-
ings, more automobiles and radios than any other civilization, but...it is superior if it produces better men and
more saints.[1]

—Fulton Sheen, *The Cross and the Crisis*

One day when Fulton Sheen was nine years old, he
noticed geranium plants for sale for ten cents outside of
a grocery store. Recalling that his mother was fond of
geraniums, he snatched one of the flowers from a plant and took
it home to his mother as a present.

Surprised by this gesture, Fulton's mother asked if he had stolen
the flower. Fulton answered affirmatively. Mrs. Sheen immediately
instructed Fulton to get fifty cents from his piggy bank and take
it to the storekeeper. Fulton protested, pointing out that a whole
plant cost only ten cents, and he had taken only one flower from
the plant. But his mother insisted, and young Fulton obeyed.[2] It
was a lesson in honesty and on the importance of restitution.

There is no greater pursuit in life than holiness. And holiness
consists not of heroic deeds but of living each moment according

to the Gospel. A stolen geranium flower may seem trivial, yet our Lord reminds us, "he who is faithful in a very little is faithful also in much; and he who is dishonest in a very little is dishonest also in much" (Luke 16:10).

Perhaps the chief menace of society is not the threat of nuclear arms or biochemical warfare but the lack of spiritual maturity, the lack of an authentic vision of the importance of holiness of life. Sheen would concur: "The dichotomy affecting the modern world is, in fact, a symptom of the deeper dichotomy that is in man himself."[3] He observes, "The world today is suffering from a terrible nemesis of mediocrity. We are dying of ordinariness; we are perishing from our pettiness. The world's greatest need is great men.... [W]hat we need are saints, for saints are the truly great men."[4]

The pursuit of holiness ought to be the single most important issue in any person's life, since in the final analysis, it is all that really matters. Yet in today's secular society, the reality of God is challenged, and the urgency of our supernatural vocation to holiness is dismissed as mere pious talk and old-fashioned belief. This present chapter will focus on Sheen's insights on our universal call to holiness, a theme that can be found in one form or another in every one of Sheen's written works.

O HAPPY FAULT!

When God created Adam and Eve, he gifted them with a share in his own inner life, which we call sanctifying grace. Not only did they live in a terrestrial paradise, but they had a foretaste of heavenly glory through the experience of holiness that radiated from within them. But one day "some one on a tree told [them] that to be like God was to be independent of God."[5] Through their decision to accept this falsehood by eating of the forbidden fruit, original sin entered the world, and thus, men and women would no longer enter the world in a state of grace.

Sheen writes, "Christianity does not begin in comfort but in catastrophe."[6] Just as death entered humanity because man listened to the voice from the tree in Eden, life would be offered when "some One else on the Tree of the Cross told him [man] that to be like God was to be dependent on Him like a son."[7] In God's wonderful plan, he offered the possibility of redemption from sin by reversing what took place in Eden at the beginning.

> There were four elements which contributed to our fall: a disobedient man, Adam; a proud woman, Eve; a tree; and the fruit of the tree. Now, only God in His sweet revenge can use the instruments of ruin as the instruments of reparation, and in His Supreme Wisdom He chose the same four: an obedient man, Christ; a humble virgin, Mary; a tree, the cross; the fruit of the tree, Christ and the Eucharist.[8]

The universal call to holiness is nothing less than God's summons to all of humanity to a life of eternal beatitude. God does not issue this invitation only to certain people but to every human being, as Scripture states: "This is good, and it is acceptable in the sight of God our Savior, *who desires all men to be saved* and to come to the knowledge of the truth" (1 Timothy 2:3–4, emphasis added). Truly, "God is more anxious to save us than we are to save ourselves,"[9] and he has given us all the means required to embrace him and abide in him unconditionally (see John 15). Only one thing is needed: our consent, which must be re-ratified every day, through every choice we make.

THE REDUCTION OF GOD

In our fallen world, our willingness to respond to God's invitation to fellowship is often inconsistent. The result is a world of crime, poverty, oppression, and a host of other physical and spiritual ills. One reason why the call to holiness is not taken as seriously as it ought to be is an incomplete understanding of God, supported by some who view him as an inconvenient truth. Sheen writes:

> There is a growing tendency in contemporary philosophy to present a religion without God. This is done either by denying God altogether, which is rare, or else by emptying the God-idea of all traditional content and identifying it with anything...as vaporous as "society divinized."[10]

Before long, and even if not explicitly stated, this reduction of God results in the elimination of God altogether. The Second Vatican Council classified the relatively recent rise of atheistic movements as "among the most serious problems of this age."[11] Indeed, the ancient world had no counterpart with a scope anywhere near that of today's atheistic movements. Most people believed in some type of divinity, while in our day, the number of persons who are either agnostic or atheist is not negligible.

The sympathy and support that atheistic movements receive is puzzling, since atheism goes against human reason; it is an irrational position. The *Catechism of the Catholic Church* states,

> Human intelligence is surely already capable of finding a response to the question of origins. The existence of God the Creator can be known with certainty through his works, by the light of human reason, even if this knowledge

is often obscured and disfigured by error. (CCC 286; see Vatican Council I, canon 2; Romans 1:19–20)

Sheen asks:

> Why is it that society would consider me insane if I spent myself and was spent in the campaign against cows that jumped over the moon, and yet would not consider the atheist insane, because he carries on a campaign to prove that God belongs to that same class of fancies and imaginings?[12]

Elsewhere Sheen bemoans the hostile social and political climate in which "God has been dethroned, the heavens emptied and man...exalted to His place in fulfillment of an evil prophecy that some day he would be like unto God."[13]

And so our initial task as evangelizers is to present the truth of God's existence. Once people accept this truth by reason, entrust themselves to God through faith, and decide to cooperate with his grace, the pursuit of sanctification can begin in earnest. The path to holiness can become a real goal in their hearts and minds.

WORLDLY PURSUITS

A second reason for a lukewarm response to our call to holiness is a preoccupation with the terrestrial over the heavenly. Many people seem more concerned about studying scientific theories than contemplating divine truths. Sheen writes, "There is nothing wrong in seeking the missing link, but it does seem to be a rather absurd emphasis on the wrong thing. Why should we be so concerned about the link which binds us to the beast, and so little concerned about the link which binds us to God?"[14]

Elsewhere he reflects:

> The source of our dignity is not to be sought by looking
> for *a man in a tree* but rather by looking to the *Man on
> the Tree*. The man in the tree is the beast swinging from
> his tail in the selfish joy of his bestiality. The Man on
> the Tree is Jesus Christ in the ecstatic beatification of His
> redemption.[15]

Sheen certainly respects and even praises science—he wrote
Philosophy of Science in 1934—but he reminds us that we must
establish the proper priorities. The divine always takes precedence
over the merely human.

Other worldly preoccupations are politics and economics. Too
many people "are still assuming with Marx that man is essentially
economic, or with Darwin that he is essentially animal, or with
Freud that he is essentially sexual, or with Hitler that he is essentially political."[16] While it is true that man's existence includes,
economic, biological, and political realms, the fact is that man
is not determined by these factors. Rather he is self-determining
through his choices. "Hence the most perfect gift we can give to
God is the gift of our will. The giving of that gift to God is the
greatest defeat that one can suffer in the eyes of the world, but it
is the greatest victory we can win in the eyes of God."[17]

Our Lord does not promise us abiding happiness without
sorrows in this life, but he will certainly endow our lives with
a thrilling sense of spiritual adventure as he transforms us to
become more like him. Sheen puts it this way:

> The continuing love of Christ does not allow our present
> way of life to come to a full stop. He always is changing

punctuation marks: He changes periods into commas....

Our present state is not so definitive that it cannot be changed. And when the period is changed into a comma by giving ourselves completely to Christ, then our lives end with an exclamation point![18]

As part of the Christian worldview, one must understand that "in the broad sense of the term, everything in the world is a sacrament, for everything in the world can be made a means of leading us on to Christ and hastening the reign of Christ."[19] Sheen points out that "there is nothing so base or low that it cannot be reconquered,...no duty however menial that cannot be retrieved for sanctity,...nothing that is cast down that cannot be lifted up."[20]

Precious is the slightest gift of supernatural grace: "All the beauties of nature do not compare in the smallest degree with the beauty of a soul in the state of grace."[21] Yet holiness does not only affect us as persons; it also sanctifies the universe. Just as sin is far-reaching in its effects, so also grace is expansive and all-encompassing in its distribution and application.

GRACE ENGAGED

You might wonder, "How does grace work? How do we gain holiness and grow in it?"

As stated earlier, we collectively forfeited divine grace through the individual choices of Adam and Eve. However, we have the opportunity to regain that divine life through the death and resurrection of Jesus Christ. Referencing this salvific event, Sheen writes, "The work of acquiring Divine life for man is finished, but not the distribution.... He has finished the foundation; we must build upon it."[22]

Through the sacrament of baptism, we appropriated for ourselves (through our sponsors, if we were baptized as babies) the graces that Jesus gained for the entire human race on Calvary. "The Sacrifice of the Cross was complete and perfect in itself. It is not complete as regards us; the merits of that great redemptive act have to flow unto us."[23]

Once we are baptized, as long as we stay away from serious sin, we abide in the sanctifying grace of God. Just as "if a farmer does not plant wheat he will not have a barren field in the fall; he will have weeds,"[24] so too is it the case that if we do not move forward in the spiritual life, we will go backward. There can be no neutrality in the spiritual life. As Jesus told us, "He who is not with me is against me" (Matthew 12:30).

One powerful guide that God gave us to help us advance on the path of virtue is our moral conscience. It is a veritable compass, a moral GPS, a built-in spiritual antenna that helps us to discern what is truly good so that we can pursue it. Sheen used a government analogy to explain this:

> Conscience is an interior government, exercising the same functions as all human government, namely, legislative, executive, and judicial. It has its Congress, its President, and its Supreme Court: it makes its laws, it witnesses our action in relation to the laws, and finally it judges us.[25]

Thirty years after Sheen penned those words, the Second Vatican Council reflected:

> In the depths of his conscience, man detects a law which he does not impose upon himself, but which holds him to obedience. Always summoning him to love good and

22

avoid evil, the voice of conscience when necessary speaks to his heart: do this, shun that. For man has in his heart a law written by God; to obey it is the very dignity of man; according to it he will be judged [see Romans 2:15–16]. Conscience is the most secret core and sanctuary of a man. There he is alone with God, Whose voice echoes in his depths.[26]

It is not always easy to make a right decision, given the many voices expressing other viewpoints. Many people, including notable public figures, claim to be Catholic and yet do not agree with or uphold the Church's basic teachings on a wide variety of moral issues, including abortion, contraception, and homosexuality. Sometimes one can hear it said that perhaps the Church needs to ease up on its moral doctrine, lest it lose a sizeable number of its members to Protestantism. In response, Sheen states, "Numbers mean little to the Church, but spirituality means everything. It may very well be, then, that God is preparing the Church for the future battle or future peace by a spiritual purification in which only the strong will walk with Him."[27]

NO GREATER LOVE

Having explored some of the basic principles behind our call to holiness, one may ask how any of this concerns our neighbor, that is, our fellow human beings. We are the ones baptized; we are the ones who make daily choices to cooperate with God or not; we are the ones who inform and follow our consciences. Is there anything we can do to help others in *their* pursuit of holiness?

The answer is a clear and resounding yes, and it can be lived out by both prayer and sacrifice. St. James tells us, "The prayer of a righteous man has great power in its effects" (James 5:16). Sheen relates this to the spiritual life using a medical analogy: "If one member [of the Mystical Body] slip[s], another runs to help him up; if it is possible to graft skin, is it not also possible to graft prayer; if it is possible to transfuse blood, is it not also possible to transfuse sacrifice?"[28]

As for distractions that may disturb our prayer at one point or another, Sheen's advice is not to worry but simply to regain focus. He shares a humorous story on the issue:

> St. Bernard had a friend once who told him he never had any distractions. St. Bernard confessed to having trouble with them. The two were out horseback riding when St. Bernard said, "I will give you this horse if you can say the Our Father without distraction. Now, get off your horse and say the Our Father." His friend got as far as the words, "Give us this day our daily bread," when he looked up at St. Bernard and asked, "Can I have the saddle too?"[29]

The application of prayer and sacrifice for our neighbor takes on even greater urgency when we consider humanity as a whole. Our neighbors include all of society, and indeed there are large-scale ramifications of the lack of the sense of the divine and holy. Sheen reminds us that "it was intended that no particular religion should be the national religion [of America], but it was never intended that the nation should be devoid of religion."[30] He warns about what will happen if a significant number of our government officials—judges, politicians, and so forth—are chosen from among the irreligious:

When we deny God as the foundation of our rights, we shall no longer have rights. The Declaration of Independence, I repeat, is a Declaration of Dependence. We are independent of dictators because we are dependent on God.

...The choice is clear: We will as a nation either go back to God and the moral law and faith in Christ, or we will rot from within. In exiling God from our national life, our politics, our economics, and our education, it was not His Heart we pierced—it was America we slew! May God forgive us![31]

The Second Vatican Council taught that "only in the mystery of the incarnate Word does the mystery of man take on light."[32] About fifteen years earlier, Sheen wrote, "It is a strange paradox, but a true one, nevertheless, that man only becomes most human when he becomes most divine, because he has been destined from all eternity to be conformable to the image of the Son of God."[33] Hence, Sheen could reflect, "She [the Church] is summoned forth to battle not for the freedom of *a man to be a saint*, but for the freedom of a man *to be a man*."[34]

To become holy is not something we do apart from daily living; rather, we pursue and attain holiness in and through our daily activities. The more we grow in holiness, actualizing our vocation to be saints, the more human we truly become. Sadly, the reverse is also true: The more we turn away from God in our personal and private lives, the less human we become. We begin a descent to the level of beasts.

In summary, Sheen reminds us that the universal call to holiness is an invitation God issues to every one of us for our eternal happiness. As the members of the Church, we should pray each day that we may accept the graces God wills for us, and we should pray that even the most obstinate sinners will allow God to enter into their lives. Through the sacraments of the Church, prayer, and sacrifice, and with an informed conscience, let us, like Fulton Sheen, go out and make disciples of every nation. Let us begin with our own sincere conversion in faith.

POINTS TO PONDER:

- What factors in your life detract from the sense of the holy? What can you do about these to establish the primacy of holiness in your life?
- In what ways, however subtle, can you raise awareness of the importance of daily sanctification in your workplace and among your friends and family?
- What factors in your life (persons, places, activities) inspire you to grow in holiness?
- Do you have a living role model who inspires virtue and holiness of life? What makes this person spiritually attractive?
- Is there a certain saint who inspires you? If so, what have you learned about the saint's life and practice of the virtues that you can imitate?
- How do you teach the importance of becoming saints to your children? If you do not have children, are there other young people in your life whom you can guide toward a virtuous life?

On Suffering and Death

He [Adam] stumbled upon the limp form of his son Abel, picked him up, carried him upon his shoulders, and laid him on the lap of Eve. They spoke to him, but Abel did not answer. He had never been so silent before. They lifted his hand, but it fell back limp; it had never acted that way before. They looked into his eyes—cold, glassy, mysteriously elusive; they had never been so unresponsive before.... *It was the first death in the world.*[1]

—Fulton Sheen, *The Seven Last Words*

The most difficult and enduring suffering experienced by Fulton Sheen was his ten-year persecution at the hands of his immediate superior, Cardinal Francis Spellman of the archdiocese of New York. It had been Spellman's initiative to propose Msgr. Sheen as a bishop, and by all accounts, Spellman intended to train Sheen as his future successor as the cardinal archbishop of New York, the most powerful position in the Catholic Church in America. But by 1957, the two had become bitterly opposed to one another.

The conflict was due to Sheen's refusal to hand over control of funds he oversaw for the Society of the Propagation of the Faith. As one of Sheen's biographers noted, "Francis Cardinal

Spellman—long-time personal friend of the Pope, ally of major political and governmental figures in the United States, a potent force in the mass media, and head of the richest diocese in the world—was a man accustomed to getting his way."[2] Yet Sheen felt it was immoral to allow funds intended for the world's poor to go toward Spellman's purposes. Spellman declared war. He appealed to the pope but lost. He told Sheen, "I will get even with you. It may take six months or ten years, but everyone will know what you're like."[3]

It was no coincidence that Sheen left television while still enjoying high ratings in 1957, nor that he was transferred from the archdiocese to the diocese of Rochester several years later and was therefore denied prospects of the cardinal's red hat as successor to Spellman. Sheen frankly admitted to a friend in 1974 that "Spellman had gotten rid of him."[4]

It was during this difficult time in his life that Sheen wrote his most successful book, *Life of Christ*. And despite the psychological and emotional suffering caused by his former mentor, Sheen never publicly spoke ill of Cardinal Spellman. Even in his autobiography, written just before his death, Sheen did not write directly about this matter. His only mention of Spellman was positive.

THIS ROTTEN WORLD

In order to appreciate the "Good News," that is, the Gospel of Jesus Christ, we first need to reflect on the "bad news" concerning human existence—namely, sin, suffering, and death. Again, Archbishop Sheen reminds us, "Christianity does not begin in comfort but in catastrophe. Once the soul begins to realize that the world is rotten because it has broken the moral law of God, it has taken the first step toward conversion."[5]

This negative dimension of human life was never intended by God but was set into motion through the abuse of human freedom and responsibility by our first parents, Adam and Eve. The Church clearly teaches this.

> *Death is a consequence of sin.* The Church's Magisterium, as authentic interpreter of the affirmations of Scripture and Tradition, teaches that death entered the world on account of man's sin. Even though man's nature is mortal God had destined him not to die. Death was therefore contrary to the plans of God the Creator and entered the world as a consequence of sin. (CCC 1008; see Genesis 2:17; 3:3, 19; Wisdom 1:13; 2:23–24; Romans 5:12; 6:23)

We, not God, are the ones responsible for this "catastrophe" of suffering and death. As Sheen states it, "The world is full of poetry; it is sin which turns it into prose."[6]

Yet, good Christians may ask why God, who is both all-good and all-powerful, allows suffering and death to endure in the world, especially after sending his Son to redeem it. Sheen observes, "There are only two things that could possibly remove evil and suffering from the world: either the conformity of human wills to the will of God, or God becoming a dictator and destroying all human wills."[7] The first option requires all of humanity to cooperate with God's grace and produce a veritable heaven on earth, an option Satan renders virtually impossible. The second option is even less possible, since God will never annul the gift of free will he has given to us.

Sheen highlights the inescapable dimension of suffering as part of our lives and compares it with our coming to a crossroads, one road of which we must take: "The first road is filled with thorns, but if we traverse it far enough, we find it ends in a bed of roses; the other road is filled with roses, but if we traverse it far enough, it ends in a bed of thorns."[8]

Sheen draws attention to the relationship between our capacity for suffering and our capacity for pleasure: "It is a remarkable fact that our sensibilities are more developed for pain than for pleasure, and our power for suffering is in excess of our power for joy."[9] He offers an explanation for this phenomenon:

> Now why is it that we have greater resources for pain than for pleasure? The real reason is this: if we live our lives as God intended that we should, then we shall leave pain behind in this world and enjoy everlasting bliss in the next. Pleasure is reserved for the next world; that is why it plays traitor to us here. Pain is not intended for the next world; that is why we can exhaust it here. Pain exists in the next world only for those who refuse to exhaust it here as an exchange for everlasting life.[10]

Thus we are able to make sense of Sheen's analogy of the crossroads: Suffering is only half of the picture; the other half of the picture is the resurrection. We all seek the latter, but to get there, we, like Christ, must pass through the former. "Unless there is a Good Friday in our lives, there will never be an Easter Sunday; unless there is a cross, there will never be an empty tomb; unless there is the torn flesh, there will never be the glorified body."[11]

The question is not whether or not we will suffer. Jesus told his disciples, "If they persecuted me, they will persecute you" (John 15:20). Sheen observes, "The truer the Church is to Christ, the greater will be her tribulation."[12] This is becoming obvious in our secular and relativistic society today.

Two Thieves

Pope St. John Paul II keenly observed that "people react to suffering in different ways. But in general it can be said that almost always the individual enters suffering with a *typically human protest* and *with the question 'why.'*"[13] We ask ourselves that question in the hope of finding a consoling answer, and that answer must begin with this central affirmation of faith: The key to unlocking the value of suffering and death is found in the suffering and death of the Son of God. John Paul II explains:

> Human suffering has reached its culmination in the Passion of Christ. And at the same time it has entered into a completely new dimension and a new order: *it has been linked to love....*
>
> In the Cross of Christ not only is the Redemption accomplished through suffering, but *also human suffering itself has been redeemed.*[14]

Suffering can either lead us to bitterness or inflame us with a sense of the divine. A concrete illustration of this can be seen in the attitudes of the two thieves who were crucified with Jesus on Good Friday. Both suffered excruciating pain. For one of the bandits, the immense suffering intensified his hatred, and he lashed out at Jesus with mocking words: "Are you not the Christ? Save yourself and us!" (Luke 23:39).

Sheen comments, "He could not assimilate pain; it came to him like [a] foreign substance to the stomach that could not digest it.

The result was that he intensified his rebellion to a point where his mouth became a crater of hate and a volcano of blasphemy."[15]

But intense suffering had a different effect on the other bandit. His suffering was a vehicle for realizing the true divinity of Jesus. It led to sorrow over his sinful life. St. Luke tells us:

> But the other [the "good thief"] rebuked him [the unrepentant bandit], saying, "Do you not fear God, since you are under the same sentence of condemnation? And we indeed justly; for we are receiving the due reward of our deeds; but this man has done nothing wrong." And he said, "Jesus, remember me when you come in your kingly power." (Luke 23:40–42)

Of this thief, Sheen writes, "The thief looked at the crown of thorns and saw there a royal diadem; the nail was to him as a scepter of power and authority; His crucifixion was His installation, and His blood, the royal purple. He asked only to be remembered."[16] Elsewhere Sheen observes, "It was the thief's last prayer, perhaps also his first.... May we not say that the thief died a thief, for he stole Paradise? Paradise can be stolen again."[17]

Consistent with this analysis, it would seem that the following words of Pope St. John Paul II could also be applied to the good thief:

> Down through the centuries and generations it has been seen that *in suffering there is concealed* a particular *power that draws a person interiorly close to Christ*, a special grace. To this grace many saints, such as Saint Francis of Assisi, Saint Ignatius of Loyola and others, owe their profound conversion. A result of such a conversion is not

only that the individual discovers the salvific meaning of suffering but above all that he becomes a completely new person. He discovers a new dimension, as it were, of *his entire life and vocation....*[18]

Sheen further observes:

Note that there were two attitudes in the soul of that thief, both of which made him acceptable to our Lord. The first was the recognition of the fact that he deserved what he was suffering, but that the sinless Christ did not deserve His Cross; in other words, he was *penitent.* The second was *faith* in Him whom men rejected, but whom the thief recognized as the very King of Kings.[19]

Sheen adds, "The thief on the left asked to be taken down, but not the thief on the right. Why? Because he knew there were greater evils than crucifixions and another life beyond the cross."[20] Indeed, "If that thief did not see purpose in pain, he would never have saved his soul. Pain can be the death of our soul, or it can be its life."[21]

John Paul II expressed the matter in this way: "It is suffering, more than anything else, which clears the way for the grace which transforms human souls. Suffering, more than anything else, makes present in the history of humanity the powers of the Redemption."[22]

TAKE UP YOUR CROSS

These reflections offer insight as to why God allows suffering and death in our world: God allows suffering because it can be a powerful instrument for our conversion and sanctification, and

God allows death because through it we are able to enter into eternal life. Sheen explains the fruitfulness of suffering in this way: "*It is God who gives us the Cross. And it is the Cross that gives us God.*"[23]

It is not enough to acknowledge mentally that suffering is allowed by God in order to bring about a greater purpose. We must link the head with the heart in understanding that we must expect to suffer, as Jesus indicated: "He who does not take his cross and follow me is not worthy of me" (Matthew 10:38). What type of cross should we expect?

Sheen responds, "There are...as many kinds of crosses as there are persons: crosses of grief and sorrow, crosses of want, crosses of abuse, crosses of wounded love and crosses of defeat."[24] Not only does everyone in the world have a cross to bear, but every cross is custom-tailored for us by the divine carpenter. No two crosses are exactly alike.[25]

Even the cross of another can have tremendous power in our own transformation. Sheen tells a story to illustrate this:

A certain juvenile delinquent immunized himself from every good influence and sought every occasion to manifest antisocial behavior. No teaching or pleading could touch his calloused heart. But he had one pet, a dog. One day, as he was teaching the dog to do a trick, he became angry because the dog did not obey him. Like all who take out their own sins on others, the boy, with a steel-shod shoe, kicked the dog in the mouth and made it bleed. When the boy ordered the dog to try the trick again, the dog first put his jaw up to the boy, then with blood-stained tongue tried to lick the master's hand; the boy broke down. Something that beatings, coaxings, restrictions could not do, suffering love did: it broke him. The Cross with its unmasked love of pain can unmask the impure pain caused by our rebellious wills.[26]

A striking feature of every Catholic Church is the crucifix over the altar. It is a crucifix, not a bare cross, for in the suffering body of the Lord, the Catholic sees the true value of suffering. And there we can fruitfully ponder St. Paul's words to the Colossians: "Now I rejoice in my sufferings for your sake, and in my flesh I complete what is lacking in Christ's afflictions for the sake of his body, that is, the church" (Colossians 1:24).

Commenting on this text, Pope John Paul II wrote:

> In this redemptive suffering, through which the Redemption of the world was accomplished, Christ opened himself from the beginning to every human suffering and constantly does so. Yes, it seems to be part of *the very essence of Christ's redemptive suffering* that this suffering requires to be unceasingly completed.... It is precisely *the Church*, which ceaselessly draws on the infinite resources of the Redemption, introducing it into the life of humanity, *which is the dimension* in which the redemptive suffering of Christ can be constantly completed by the suffering of man.[27]

John Paul II affirmed the fact that indeed the sacrifice of Jesus was perfect, lacking nothing in degree. At the same time, he confirmed that we need to "complete" the sufferings of Christ in our own sufferings, which we endure with him and through him. Archbishop Sheen explains that Jesus "can never again suffer in His own human nature.... He therefore has willed to prolong His loving passion unto the end of the world by perpetuating it in the members of his Mystical Body."[28]

Again, Pope John Paul II observed:

> The Redeemer suffered in place of man and for man. Every man has *his own share in the Redemption.* Each one is also *called to share in that suffering* through which the Redemption was accomplished. He is called to share in that suffering through which all human suffering has also been redeemed. In bringing about the Redemption through suffering, Christ *has* also *raised human suffering to the level of the Redemption.* Thus each man, in his suffering, can also become a sharer in the redemptive suffering of Christ.[29]

Sheen tells us that "the Cross is the problem of pain and death; but the Crucifix is the solution."[30] That is:

> The Crucifix does not mean pain; it means sacrifice. In other words, it tells us, first, pain is sacrifice without love; and secondly, that sacrifice is pain with love.
>
> ...Love is the only force in the world which can make pain bearable, and it makes it more than bearable by transforming it into the joy of sacrifice.[31]

Attempting to separate Christ from the cross earned Peter a harsh rebuke from Jesus (see Matthew 16:21–23), yet in God's sweet irony, "*The man who tempted the Lord away from the cross was the first apostle to embrace it himself.*"[32] Sheen warns us that "Satan comes without a cross, and not until victims are his do they know that the greatest cross in life is not to have the Cross."[33]

FORGIVING

What should our attitude be toward those who have a hand in our sufferings? We find our answer in the attitude of Jesus Christ:

> At that very moment when a tree turns against Him and becomes a cross, when iron turns against Him and becomes nails, when roses turn against Him and become thorns, when men turn against Him and become executioners, He lets fall from His lips for the first time in the history of the world a prayer for enemies: "Father, forgive them, for they know not what they do" (Luke 23:34).[34]

So many times we experience suffering as without meaning because it does not occur to us to "offer it up" for our own sins and the sins of the Mystical Body of Christ. Sheen laments, "The greatest tragedy of life is not what happens to souls, but rather what souls miss.... There is nothing more tragic in all the world than wasted pain."[35]

Similarly, "death is a terrible thing for him who dies only when he dies; but it is a beautiful thing for him who dies before he dies."[36] By this Sheen means that every time we accept our sufferings and unite them to Christ's passion, we die "little deaths" that prepare our hearts and minds to be properly disposed to accept, rather than to fear, our own death when it finally comes. Whereas the cross was man's judgment on Christ and, by extension, on all who follow Christ, the empty tomb is God's judgment on Christ and on those worthy to be called Christians.[37]

In summary, the problem of suffering and death is real. May we take consolation in the fact that the only reason God allows it is to transform our sinful ways into paths of virtue and charity. As the two bandits who were crucified next to Jesus show, suffering can make us bitter or can lead us to the divine.

May we never lose hope or be discouraged by suffering. For if we see and accept the redemptive meaning of human suffering, "the sinner of this hour might be the saint of the next."[38]

POINTS TO PONDER

- God calls us to trust in him in the midst of our suffering, but sometimes he allows us to understand the good that comes from it. Do you recognize the good that came from a certain suffering in your life?

- Pope St. John Paul II alluded to St. Francis of Assisi and St. Ignatius of Loyola as men who gained spiritual clarity through suffering. Do you know their stories? Are there other saints with whom you can identify when you undergo suffering?

- Do you know someone who experienced a recent tragedy? What can you say or do for that person? What should you not say or do?

- Do you have faith that through death you can enter eternal life? Do you still fear death? If so, why?

The Sacrament of Confession

A few decades ago, nobody believed in the confession of sins except the Church. Today everyone believes in confession, with this difference: Some believe in confessing their own sins; others believe in confessing other people's sins.[1]

—Fulton Sheen, *Peace of Soul*

In his autobiography, Sheen recounts the story of a young woman who came to him for confession only because her mother insisted that she go. The woman started out by making small talk with Sheen in the confessional. She acknowledged that she was afraid to make a true confession. For the next twenty minutes, Sheen begged her to tell him the reason for her fear. She refused and left the confessional.

Sheen encountered the woman again on the steps of the church. For another thirty minutes, he begged her to give him the reason why she would not make a good confession. She finally explained that she had made a pact with the devil to make nine sacrilegious Communions, which she already had fulfilled. Then the woman ran away.

Sheen returned to the church and asked every penitent in line to pray a rosary "for the conversion of a sinner." After hearing confessions, he spent three and a half hours in prayer within the church for this woman's conversion. Then the door of the church opened, and the young woman entered. She walked directly into the confessional and made a good confession.[2]

GRACE FOR SINNERS

Often we hear non-Catholics say that Christians do not need to confess sins to a priest in order to be forgiven; all we must do is pray to God for forgiveness in the privacy of our own soul. Why confess our sins to another fallible human being, one who could have committed sins much worse than our own? Is it not only God who forgives sin? What biblical basis is there for confessing sins to a representative of the Church?

The Catholic Church recognizes the sacrament of confession, also called the sacrament of penance or reconciliation, as one of the seven supernatural means given to humanity by Jesus Christ himself to aid us in our pilgrimage toward eternal life.

> Christ instituted the sacrament of Penance for all sinful members of his Church: above all for those who, since Baptism, have fallen into grave sin, and have thus lost their baptismal grace and wounded ecclesial communion. It is to them that the sacrament of Penance offers a new possibility to convert and to recover the grace of justification. The Fathers of the Church present this sacrament as "the second plank [of salvation] after the shipwreck which is the loss of grace."[47] (CCC 1446, citing Tertullian, *De Pœnitentia* 4, 2: PL 1, 1343, and the Council of Trent [1547]: DS 1542)

The *Catechism* goes on to point out that "after having attained the age of discretion, each of the faithful is bound by an obligation faithfully to confess serious sins at least once a year" (CCC 1457). Also, one must be in the state of grace to receive Communion, so "anyone aware of having sinned mortally must not receive communion without having received absolution in the sacrament of penance" (CCC 1415).

There is no strict requirement to avail oneself of the sacrament of confession if one remains free of mortal sin (see CCC 1458). Here the non-Catholic is correct: It is possible to receive God's forgiveness by praying to God directly and expressing sorrow for our sin. Yet, every sacrament confers grace to empower us to grow in holiness and love for God and one another.

Pope St. John Paul II stressed the wisdom of confessing even our venial sins in order to gain true freedom from sin:

> We shall also do well to recall that, for a balanced spiritual and pastoral orientation in this regard, great importance must continue to be given to teaching the faithful also to make use of the sacrament of penance for venial sins alone, as is borne out by a centuries-old doctrinal tradition and practice.
>
> Though the church knows and teaches that venial sins are forgiven in other ways too,...she does not cease to remind everyone of the special usefulness of the sacramental moment for these sins too. The frequent use of the sacrament...strengthens the awareness that even minor sins offend God and harm the church, the body of Christ.... Above all it should be emphasized that the grace proper to the sacramental celebration has a great remedial power and helps to remove the very roots of sin.[3]

The *Catechism of the Catholic Church* explains some of the benefits of confessing minor sins:

> Indeed the regular confession of our venial sins helps us form our conscience, fight against evil tendencies, let ourselves be healed by Christ and progress in the life of the Spirit. By receiving more frequently through this sacrament the gift of the Father's mercy, we are spurred to be merciful as he is merciful. (CCC 1458)

It is important to understand that in the sacrament of confession, God is the one forgiving the sins. He chooses to do it through his ordained priests. Sheen explains, "Man cannot forgive sins, but God can forgive sins through man."[4]

WHY GO TO CONFESSION?

Archbishop Sheen addresses some of the reasons why confession of sins to a priest is essential. First, he emphasizes the fact that the priest is a mediator of divine grace, not some obstacle to a personal encounter with God.

> Why should a confessor stand between my God and me? For the same reason that the human nature of Christ stands between His divinity and me.... [B]eing made up as we are of body and soul, it is fitting that [a] body or a human nature be the means by which we commune with God.[5]

We do not need to escape from our humanity in order to share in God's divinity. Rather, it is in and through humanity that we are able to receive divine grace and advance toward heavenly glory. This is particularly true of the humanity configured to the priesthood of Christ through the sacrament of holy orders.

Human persons are not simply bodies or souls but rather body-soul composites. When we sin, it is not the body alone that sins, nor the spirit alone, but all of man—the "I." The work of redemption accomplished by Christ affects the entire person, the body-soul composite that constitutes the "me." When we go to confession, our whole self is able to be restored to communion with God through the mediation of another whole self configured to be a dispenser of God's mercy through priestly ordination.

Sheen's incarnation analogy illustrates the priest's role as mediator between God and man. When we consider the relationship between the two natures of Jesus Christ, we observe that the human nature is the bridge to encountering his divinity. While he was on earth, Jesus forgave sins through his human nature.[6] Sheen explains:

> The divine life of Christ is communicated through His Church or His Mystical Body in exactly the same way that His divine life was communicated when He walked on earth. As He then used His human nature as the instrument of divinity, and used material things as signs and symbols of the conferring of His pardon, so He now uses other human natures and material things as the instruments for the communication of that same divine life.[7]

A second reason Sheen provides to explain why we confess our sins to a priest is related to the summons to express perfect sorrow, called contrition, after offending God. Sheen writes:

> It may be asked, why did Our Lord demand a telling of sins? Why not bury one's head in one's handkerchief,

and tell God that one is sorry?... Shedding tears in one's handkerchief is no test of sorrow, because we are then the judges. Who would ever be sentenced to prison, if every man were his own judge? How easy it would be for murderers and thieves to escape justice and judgment simply by having a handkerchief ready![8]

A third reason Sheen gives us for the confession of sins to a priest is the corrective to pride and cultivation of humility it provides. He describes pride as the chief among the seven "pallbearers of a soul"[9] and points out what happens to it in the sacrament of confession: "Because sin is pride, it demands a humiliation, and there is no greater humiliation than unburdening one's soul to a fellow man."[10]

A fourth reason for confessing our sins to a priest is that "every sin is an offense, not against God alone, but also against our neighbor.... And since every sin is an offense against the love of God and brotherhood of Christ, it follows that a representative of that spiritual fellowship should, in God's name, and through God's power, receive the individual back into the fellowship."[11]

Sheen observes, "When we do evil, or commit sin, we affect every member of the Church in some way. This is even done in our most secret sins."[12] John Paul II explained the matter in this way:

One cannot deny the social nature of this sacrament, in which the whole church—militant, suffering and glorious in heaven—comes to the aid of the penitent and welcomes him again into her bosom, especially as it was the whole church which had been offended and wounded by his sin. As the minister of penance, the priest by virtue of his sacred office appears as the witness and representative of this ecclesial nature of the sacrament.[13]

On a human level, only the person sinned against is capable of forgiving us of our wrongdoing. If Joe hits Tom, I cannot rightly say to Joe, "I forgive you for hitting Tom." Only Tom can do that. Since the priest represents both the vertical dimension of God's mercy and the horizontal dimension of humanity, he is capable of speaking for both.

HAPPY HEARTS

A fifth reason for the confession of sins is that it benefits our psychological health. Sheen observes, "It is not enough to diagnose a disease: it must also be cured, but there is no cure for a guilty conscience except pardon."[14] Sheen points out one of the numerous differences between visiting a priest and visiting a psychoanalyst: "It costs considerable money to tell one's complexes to a psychoanalyst; it costs only pride and arrogance of soul to confess our sins to representatives of the moral and Divine order."[15]

The Church requires that all mortal sins be confessed according to both kind and number, that is, what we did and approximately how many times we did it. By confessing the sin in this way, we take full responsibility for it and can more easily let go of all guilt associated with it. Sheen writes, "Our Divine Lord said that repression of sins was dangerous; if we covered them up, they would cause an irritation with eternal consequences. So He asked His Apostles to go around the world preventing repression by hearing confessions and forgiving sins."[16]

We all seek the peace of conscience that comes from the absolution of our sins. Sheen remarks, "When a frustrated man says he has a good conscience, he only means he has a bad memory."[17] On the other hand:

> Regular confession prevents sins, worries, and anxieties from seeping down into the unconscious and degenerating into melancholy fears and neuroses.... Our Lord knew what was in man so He instituted this sacrament, not for His needs but for ours. It was His way of giving man a happy heart.[18]

The final reason Sheen gives to support the practice of confessing sins to a priest is perhaps the most convincing, namely, the command from Jesus Christ himself:

> Jesus said to them [the apostles] again, "Peace be with you. As the Father has sent me, even so I send you." And when he had said this, he breathed on them, and said to them, "Receive the Holy Spirit. If you forgive the sins of any, they are forgiven; if you retain the sins of any, they are retained." (John 20:21–23)

Sheen comments:

> Our divine Redeemer here says that He was sent by the Father; now He sends them with the power to forgive or not forgive. These words imply "hearing confessions," because how would the priests of the Church know which sins to forgive and which sins not to forgive if they did not hear them?[19]

Pope St. John Paul II stated:

> It would therefore be foolish, as well as presumptuous, to wish arbitrarily to disregard the means of grace and

salvation which the Lord has provided and, in the specific case, to claim to receive forgiveness while doing without the sacrament which was instituted by Christ precisely for forgiveness.[20]

OBSTACLES TO CONFESSION

Given the wisdom and logic of all the reasons for regular sacramental confession, we may wonder why it is difficult for us to put them into play. Why do we hold back from the sacrament of penance?

Perhaps many of us can identify with a penitent that Sheen encountered who needed some assistance in getting to confession. The woman was a famous actress in London. She approached Sheen for spiritual advice, but she insisted on one stipulation: namely, that Sheen promise not to ask her to go to confession. Sheen agreed, though he was resolved to have her make a good confession. Sheen tells what happened next:

> That afternoon before the matinee, she returned. I then told her that we had a Rembrandt and a Van Dyck in the church: "Would you like to see them?" As we walked down the side aisle, we passed a confessional. I pushed her in. I did not ask her to go, for I had promised not to *ask* her to go. Two years later I gave her her veil in a convent in London, where she is to this very hour.[21]

Sometimes it is Satan who puts obstacles in the way of our confession. These obstacles can cause tensions within us, giving rise to an intense spiritual battle between light and darkness. God is prompting us to go to confession, while Satan attempts to dissuade us through his trickery and deception. By reflecting on some of

Satan's strategies, we can be better prepared to resist them and attain true reconciliation with God.

Let's consider the obstacle, suggested through Satan's faulty logic, that runs like this: Perhaps the priest is no saint either, so it does not make sense that one sinner would need to go to another sinner for forgiveness. Sheen counters this way of thinking with an example from the natural world: "Sunlight is not polluted by passing through a dirty window. God can write straight with crooked lines."[22]

The priest does not receive the power to forgive sins from his own humanity, nor has he merited this power. Rather, the power is given directly by God through priestly ordination, and the exercise of this divine power is completely independent of the personal holiness (or lack thereof) of the priest.

A second obstacle that may cause a sinner to shy away from the sacrament of confession is the fear of shame that may be experienced when confessing serious sins, particularly those in the realm of human sexuality. Yet such sensitive matters are often pernicious to our spiritual and emotional well-being. It is only in confessing them that healing can begin. The *Catechism of the Catholic Church* states:

> All mortal sins of which penitents after a diligent self-examination are conscious must be recounted by them in confession, even if they are most secret and have been committed against the last two precepts of the Decalogue; *for these sins sometimes wound the soul more grievously and are more dangerous than those which are committed openly.* (CCC 1456, emphasis added)

A third reason a sinner may give for avoiding confession is busyness. Perhaps we work during the times our local parish reserves for confession each week, and we never get around to making an appointment with a priest. We reduce the font of God's mercy to a mere juridical process that is just too inconvenient.

Concerning this objection, Sheen points out that "the time one has for anything depends on how much he values it."[23] If a person truly values the health of his or her immortal soul and relationship with the Almighty, then the person will be sure to find the time needed to set right what has been destroyed by sin.

One might also consider the even greater inconvenience of confession for the priest! Sheen writes:

> If the Church had invented any of the sacraments, there is one that it certainly would have done away with, and that is the Sacrament of Penance. This because of the trials that it imposes upon those who have to hear confessions, sitting in the confessional box for long hours while listening to the terrific monotony of fallen human nature.[24]

Many years later, Pope John Paul II would express similar sentiments about the priest's duty of hearing confessions: "This is undoubtedly the most difficult and sensitive, the most exhausting and demanding ministry of the priest, but also one of the most beautiful and consoling."[25]

Further, in light of the grueling, torturous passion and death of our Lord, we certainly have no grounds to dismiss as inconvenient anything that will further our salvation. Through the eyes of faith, Sheen writes, "the crucifix is an autobiography in which man can read the story of his own life, either to his own salvation or his own condemnation."[26] Elsewhere he states:

> It is not easy, indeed, for a man to make his way to the
> Cross and admit that he has been wrong. It is very hard;
> but the penitent knows that it was harder to hang on that
> Cross! We are never made worse by admitting we are
> broken-hearted, for unless our hearts are broken, how
> can God get in?[27]

In summary, the priest is the divinely chosen mediator of grace,
just as the humanity of Jesus was the channel through which his
divinity was made known. When we confess our sins to a priest,
it promotes true sorrow for sin. It also fosters a spirit of humility,
which counteracts pride, the root of all sin. The priest represents
the entire moral and spiritual order that was offended by our sin,
thereby calling to mind the communitarian dimension of both sin
and grace. Confession brings about both spiritual and psychological healing. Jesus intended that confessing one's sins to his priests
would be the normative way of receiving forgiveness of mortal
sins committed after baptism.

Do you have trouble getting to confession? I encourage you to
reflect on these reasons for the sacrament and resolve to accept
the grace God makes available through it. No obstacle is strong
enough to keep us from reconciliation with our heavenly Father.

POINTS TO PONDER

- Have you ever reflected on the gift of a second, third, or fourth
  chance? What would life be like if the graces and forgiveness of
  confession were not available to you?
- What keeps you from getting in line for confession?
- Do you prefer going to confession face-to-face or through the
  screen? Why?

- God is quick to extend his mercy and forgiveness to you. Are you willing to extend forgiveness to others? How can you share God's mercy with others?
- Have you prayed for priests today?

CHAPTER FIVE

The Eucharist

The first rupture in the soul of Judas was when Our
Lord said He would give man His Body and Blood as
their food. The total collapse came the night of the Last
Supper, when Our Blessed Lord fulfilled this promise.
Here is unmistakable evidence that fidelity and holiness
on the one hand, and betrayal and disloyalty on the other,
are linked to the Eucharist, the Bread of Life.[1]

—Fulton Sheen, *The Priest Is Not His Own*

Upon Sheen's ordination to the priesthood, he made a
strict resolution to God, as he recorded in his autobiography: "I resolved...to spend a continuous Holy Hour
every day in the presence of Our Lord in the Blessed Sacrament."[2]
At Sheen's funeral, the homilist, Archbishop Edward O'Meara,
stated, "As surely as we are here in St. Patrick's Cathedral this
afternoon, he made his Holy Hour last Sunday morning, the day
of his passing."[3]

Sometimes this Holy Hour would be more adventurous than
he could have imagined. One evening in Chicago, he went to a
church, but it was locked. He summoned the pastor, who let him
into the church and then forgot all about him. The problem was

that the locked doors not only prevented anyone from entering the church but also prevented anyone from leaving.

After completing his Holy Hour, Sheen spent a couple more hours trying to figure out how to get out of the church. He finally decided to go out through one of the church windows. He landed in the coal bin, much to the astonishment of the church's house-keeper, who heard the commotion.[4]

JESUS PRESENT

Coming from the Greek term meaning "thanksgiving," the Eucharist is the real presence of Jesus Christ—Body, Blood, soul, and divinity—under the appearances of bread and wine. It is the most central sacrament of the Christian life. The other six sacraments are extensions of God's power into space and time; only the Eucharist is God himself.[5] "The Church draws her life from the Eucharist," John Paul II wrote in his encyclical *Ecclesia de Eucharistia*.[6] The Church affirms:

> The Most Blessed Eucharist contains the entire spiritual good of the Church, that is, Christ himself, our Pasch and Living Bread, by the action of the Holy Spirit through his very flesh vital and vitalizing, giving life to men who are thus invited and encouraged to offer themselves, their labors and all created things, together with him....[7]

One overarching and vital dimension of our understanding of the Eucharist is that it is not merely a symbol of Jesus Christ but rather Jesus Christ sacramentally and truly present. A second crucial dimension of Catholic understanding is that the Eucharistic banquet is not merely a meal to be celebrated at a table but, first and foremost, a true sacrifice that finds its proper celebration at the altar. Linking these two essential dimensions of the Eucharist, Sheen writes that "the Sacrifice is first and then the Sacrament, for it was the Cross which made the Eucharist, and it is its prolongation or the Mass which makes the Communion."[8]

The sacrament of the Eucharist is brought about in the context of the Mass, "the temporalization in time and localization in space of Calvary."[9] The Mass is understood as the unbloody re-presentation of Christ's sacrifice. Jesus is not re-sacrificed at each Mass, but rather, the fruits of his one and perfect sacrifice are brought into the present. Sheen comments, "The Mass, then, is Calvary *recalled, renewed and applied.*"[10]

Sheen explains that "only sensible advantages would accrue to those who wished they had been at Calvary and the empty tomb. The same drama is repeated in the Mass, and faith interprets the event in both instances."[11] Elsewhere he reflects, "What happened there on the Cross that day is happening now in the Mass, with this difference: on the Cross the Saviour was alone; in the Mass He is with us."[12]

During the most solemn part of the Mass, the Consecration, by the power of God working through the ordained priest, the elements cease to be bread and wine and become the Body and Blood of Jesus Christ. Sheen, addressing those who—out of fear, scandal, disbelief, or some other motive—do not accept Christ's teaching about the Eucharist at face value, comments on the Bread of Life discourse in the sixth chapter of the Gospel of John:

> Christ's words were too literal, and He cleared up too many false interpretations, for any of His hearers to claim that the Eucharist (or Body and Blood He would give) was a mere type or symbol, or that its effects depended upon the subjective dispositions of the receiver. It was our

Lord's method whenever anyone *misunderstood* what He said to correct the misunderstanding, as He did when Nicodemus thought *born again* meant re-entering his mother's womb. But, whenever anyone correctly understood what He said, but found fault with it, He *repeated* what He said. And in this discourse, Our Lord repeated five times what He had said about His Body and Blood.[13]

FOOD FOR THE SOUL

One might ask why bread and wine are used by Jesus for the celebration of this sacrament, and not some other elements. Sheen comments on how fitting bread and wine are. First, these two elements are powerful symbols of ourselves: "Man has traditionally been nourished by bread and wine. When he brings that which has given him physical sustenance, he is equivalently bringing himself. He makes himself present on the altar before God."[14]

Second, these elements remind us that all of creation is good, and it is fitting to give back to God of the goodness he has given us. Third, Sheen observes, "As bread is made from a multiplicity of grains of wheat and wine from a multiplicity of grapes, so we who are many are one in Christ."[15]

Fourth, and perhaps most profoundly, Sheen asks, "Was not the wheat already broken to become bread? Were not the grapes already crushed to become wine?"[16] Here he highlights the sacrificial dimension of the Eucharist, evoking the brokenness of Christ's own body and the outpouring of his precious blood to accomplish the work of our redemption from sin.

Sheen reminds us that "the life of the body is the soul; the life of the soul is Christ."[17] We nourish our souls with the life of Christ through the worthy reception of the Eucharist. To receive the

Eucharist worthily means to be in a state of grace, that is, free of mortal sin. This is a serious obligation, Sheen reflects: "If God punished the Philistines so harshly for keeping the tabernacle, which was only a promise and prototype of the Eucharist, then what reverence should the Eucharist itself not awaken in those who have the reality and the substance!"[18]

We ought not to take lightly the admonition of St. Paul, "Whoever, therefore, eats the bread or drinks the cup of the Lord in an unworthy manner will be guilty of profaning the body and blood of the Lord" (1 Corinthians 11:27). And the *Catechism of the Catholic Church* states, "Before so great a sacrament, the faithful can only echo humbly and with ardent faith the words of the Centurion:...'Lord, I am not worthy that you should enter under my roof, but only say the word and my soul will be healed'" (CCC 1386).

The *Catechism* also reminds us that the fruits, or effects, of the Eucharist in the person who worthily receives it include intimate union with Jesus Christ, an increase in grace and strengthening of the virtues, forgiveness of venial sins, and the supernatural assistance necessary to preserve us from future sin (see CCC 1391– 1398). The Eucharist also both signifies and brings about the unity of the entire Church, the Mystical Body of Christ. Sheen teaches us, "The two words 'Mystical Body' are first actually combined by St. John Chrysostom in speaking of the Eucharist."[19]

So we must never overlook our commitment to one another, especially to the poor among us. Sheen recounts, "A dying man in a country region of France, unable to receive the Eucharist, asked that a poor person be brought to him so that he might at least have Christ in a lesser way."[20]

Perhaps we all know persons who deny the Eucharist and others who focus exclusively on the worthy sacramental reception of it. Sheen makes an observation that may startle both: "If all we did during our lives was to go to Communion, and receive Divine Life, to take it away, and leave nothing behind, we would be *parasites* on the Mystical Body of Christ."[21]

Sheen is remarkably insightful in stressing the importance of allowing the Eucharist to transform our minds and hearts after the example of Christ. Through the worthy reception of the Eucharist, we truly become what we eat. We are to "go in peace" and be witnesses of the charity of Christ to all we meet. Sheen observes, "Natural life has two sides: the anabolic and the katabolic. Supernatural life also has two sides: the building of the Christ-pattern and the tearing down of the old Adam."[22]

One comment often given by those who do not attend Mass is that the Mass is boring. To this we may ask why everything in life needs to be filled with worldly excitement. It is precisely the otherworldly dimension of the Mass, its foretaste of the heavenly wedding feast of the Lamb, that allows God to work so powerfully through it. Sheen reminds us, "Excitement is not religion; if it was, an 'Alleluia' on Sunday could become a 'Crucify' on Friday."[23]

There are some who complain that they do not get anything out of the Mass, to which Sheen responds, "True, but this is because they bring nothing to it."[24] And of course, there are Catholics who do not attend Mass because they think it is optional, an event only for Easter and Christmas. They are somehow unaware of the Church's official teaching that every Sunday is a holy day of obligation, since it commemorates the resurrection of Jesus from the dead.

EUCHARISTIC ADORATION

In addition to the reception of Holy Communion, the Church also offers to her faithful the spiritually rich practice of Eucharistic Adoration. Known also as a "Holy Hour" when the period of adoration lasts sixty minutes, Eucharistic Adoration consists of time spent in prayer before Jesus Christ in the monstrance. There our Lord is visible to us under the appearance of bread.

Pope Benedict XVI reflected on the confusion that followed the reforms of the Second Vatican Council as to whether Eucharistic Adoration was a legitimate practice: "[A]n objection that was widespread at the time argued that the Eucharistic bread was given to us not to be looked at, but to be eaten." The Holy Father continued,

> In the light of the Church's experience of prayer, however, this was seen to be a false dichotomy. As Saint Augustine put it: *"nemo autem illam carnem manducat, nisi prius adoraverit; peccemus non adorando"*—"no one eats that flesh without first adoring it; we should sin were we not to adore it." In the Eucharist, the Son of God comes to meet us and desires to become one with us; eucharistic adoration is simply the natural consequence of the eucharistic celebration, which is itself the Church's supreme act of adoration. Receiving the Eucharist means adoring him whom we receive. Only in this way do we become one with him, and are given, as it were, a foretaste of the beauty of the heavenly liturgy. The act of adoration outside Mass prolongs and intensifies all that takes place during the liturgical celebration itself....[25]

The biblical basis for the Holy Hour is our Lord's words during his agony in Gethsemane: "And he came to the disciples and found them sleeping; and he said to Peter, 'So, could you not watch with me one hour? Watch and pray that you may not enter into temptation; the spirit indeed is willing, but the flesh is weak'" (Matthew 26:40–41).

Sheen's advice as to how to spend the Holy Hour is liberating: "No rules—just spend a continuous hour before the Blessed Sacrament."[26] He acknowledges that "some spiritual writers recommend a mechanical division of the hour into four parts: thanksgiving, petition, adoration, reparation." But he adds, "This is unnecessarily artificial. An hour's conversation with a friend is not divided into four rigid segments or topics."[27]

Archbishop Sheen even has something for those of us who, despite our best efforts, may be lulled to sleep in the quiet and sometimes darkness of the Eucharistic chapel:

> I knelt down and said a prayer of adoration, and then sat down to meditate and immediately went to sleep. I woke up exactly at the end of one hour. I said to the Good Lord: "Have I made a Holy Hour?" I thought His angel said: "Well, that's the way the Apostles made their first Holy Hour in the Garden, but don't do it again."[28]

EVERY KNEE SHALL BOW

Sheen argues for the importance of kneeling before our Eucharistic Lord in a world that seems to have forgotten the meaning of worship. He cites some biblical examples to remind us of the value of kneeling in prayer: Stephen at his martyrdom (Acts 7:59-60); Peter on his knees before Jesus and before he raised Tabitha from the dead (Luke 5:8; Acts 9:40); St. Paul in prayer (Acts 20:35–36; Ephesians 3:14); the rich young man before Jesus (Mark 10:17); the soldiers mocking Jesus (Mark 15:19); Jesus praying in Gethsemane (Luke 22:41); the mother of the sons of Zebedee before Jesus (Matthew 20:20); the father of the possessed boy (Matthew 17:14); and the leper before Jesus (Mark 1:40).

Pope Benedict XVI shares Sheen's perspective on the value of kneeling:

> There is a story that comes from the sayings of the Desert Fathers, according to which the devil was compelled by God to show himself to a certain Abba Apollo. He looked black and ugly, with frighteningly thin limbs, but, most strikingly, he had no knees. The inability to kneel is seen as the very essence of the diabolical.[29]

Sheen would undoubtedly agree with the Holy Father's assessment:

> It may well be that kneeling is alien to modern culture—insofar as it is a culture, for this culture has turned away from the faith and no longer knows the One before whom kneeling is the right, indeed the intrinsically necessary gesture. The man who learns to believe learns also to kneel, and a faith or a liturgy no longer familiar with kneeling would be sick at the core.[30]

Of course, our Lord understands that sometimes due to physical hardships the body is not able to express the devotion that wells up from deep within our heart and soul. Neither Sheen nor the Church expects those with disabilities, injuries, or advancement in age to kneel.

In summary, the Eucharist is both a sacrament and a sacrifice. Since it truly is the Body, Blood, soul, and divinity of Jesus Christ, to this most august sacrament we owe our adoration. When we receive the Eucharist properly disposed, by being in the state of sanctifying grace, we receive the life of Jesus Christ into our souls, transforming us by grace through union with him. Having been fed by the Eucharist, we are commissioned to work in charity for Christian unity and to have a special predilection for the poor among us.

POINTS TO PONDER

- Is Eucharistic Adoration currently part of your spirituality? If it is, what do you do during your time before the Blessed Sacrament? If it is not, are you willing to try adding it to your prayer?
- How can you better foster awareness of and reverence for the Eucharist?
- When you prepare to receive the Eucharist at Mass, do you consciously attempt to enter into the mystery of Christ's love for you?
- The Eucharist is Christ's supreme gift to his Church, since it is the gift of himself. How can you give back to God through all that he has given to you? Can you give a gift of time, talent, or treasure to someone in the name of Jesus Christ?

CHAPTER SIX

The Priesthood

O priest, who are you? You are not from yourself, because you are from nothing. You are not to yourself, because you are a mediator to God. You are not for yourself, because you ought to live for God alone. You are not of yourself, because you are the servant of all. You are not yourself, because you are another Christ. What therefore are you? Nothing and everything, O priest![1]

—Fulton Sheen, *The Priest Is Not His Own*

J oyfully reflecting on his own ordination, Sheen compares the priesthood to a holy fraternity: "The priesthood is the greatest fraternity in the world. No introduction is necessary to another priest; there is nothing to live up to; nothing to live down. The mere fact that he is a priest means that he is a brother."[2]

Sheen began praying as a young priest that he would be ordained a bishop someday.[3] Normally, such high aspirations would speak ill of a priest, since priests ought to recognize that they are unworthy of the priesthood, let alone the fullness of the priesthood conferred through ordination to the episcopacy. But Sheen's hope stemmed from his great love for the Church and his desire to become a successor to the apostles and carry out their earthly ministry. Apostolic zeal, not pride, was the reason for his ambition.

WHO ARE YOU?

A priest is one who offers a sacrifice to God on behalf of himself and others. Jesus Christ is the perfect High Priest. He offers himself to the Father through his cross for the forgiveness of our sins. (The Letter to the Hebrews discusses this theme in detail.)

The Catholic Church acknowledges two participations in this one priesthood of Jesus Christ: the common priesthood of all the baptized and the ministerial priesthood conferred through the sacrament of holy orders. Through our baptism and confirmation, we participate in the triple office of Jesus Christ as priest, prophet, and king (see CCC 1546). Vatican II affirms:

> The baptized, by regeneration and the anointing of the Holy Spirit, are consecrated as a spiritual house and a holy priesthood, in order that through all those works which are those of the Christian man they may offer spiritual sacrifices and proclaim the power of Him who has called them out of darkness into His marvelous light. Therefore all the disciples of Christ, persevering in prayer and praising God, should present themselves as a living sacrifice, holy and pleasing to God. Everywhere on earth they must bear witness to Christ and give an answer to those who seek an account of that hope of eternal life which is in them. (*Lumen Gentium,* 10; see 1 Peter 2:4–10; Acts 2:42–47; Romans 12:1; 1 Peter 3:15)

Only through the sacrament of holy orders is a man empowered to act in the name of Christ for the good of the whole Church.

The ministerial priesthood has the task not only of representing Christ—Head of the Church— before the assembly of the faithful, but also of acting in the name of the whole Church when presenting to God the prayer of the Church, and above all when offering the Eucharistic sacrifice. (*CCC* 1552; see Vatican II, *Sacrosanctum Concilium*, 33; *Lumen Gentium*, 10)

The sacrament of holy orders "configures the recipient to Christ by a special grace of the Holy Spirit, so that he may serve as Christ's instrument for his Church. By ordination one is enabled to act as a representative of Christ, Head of the Church" (*CCC* 1581).

The two ways of participating in the priesthood of Jesus are not simply different in degree but different in their very essence.[4] A layperson cannot assume the functions proper to a priest in the priest's absence, since the ministerial grace of the Holy Spirit particular to priestly identity is conferred by the bishop through the sacrament of holy orders. The fact that a Catholic priest is not called simply by his first name, but rather referred to as "Father," signifies that the sacramental character received in holy orders causes an ontological change within the man. It is a permanent identity change.

The Priest and the Eucharist

Citing St. Thomas Aquinas, Archbishop Sheen points out that the primary and most important spiritual power of holy orders is the ability to bring about the Eucharist, that is, to take bread and wine and change it into the Body, Blood, soul, and divinity of Jesus Christ. St. Thomas Aquinas expressed it this way: "The Orders are directed to the sacrament of the Eucharist chiefly, and to the other sacraments consequently, for even the other sacraments flow from that which is contained in that sacrament."[5] All other aspects and purposes of holy orders are secondary to this primary function. Sheen observes that "all the priest's powers over the Mystical Body of Christ derive from his power over the True Body of Christ or the Eucharist."[6]

As we have seen in the previous chapter, the fall of Judas was both prefigured and brought about in the context of his denial of the Eucharist, prompting Sheen to reflect, "The moral rot of the priesthood starts with a want of lively faith in the Divine Presence, and the sanctity of the priesthood starts there too."[7]

The Second Vatican Council confirms Sheen's outlook in its Decree on the Ministry and Life of Priests:

> Through the ministry of the priests, the spiritual sacrifice of the faithful is made perfect in union with the sacrifice of Christ. He is the only mediator who in the name of the whole Church is offered sacramentally in the Eucharist and in an unbloody manner until the Lord himself comes [see 1 Corinthians 11:26]. The ministry of priests is directed to this goal and is perfected in it.[8]

This same document goes on to point out that the priest's work of proclaiming the Gospel and his apostolate of pastoral charity are also driven by the Eucharist and focused on it. It states that "the Eucharist appears as the source and the summit of all preaching of the Gospel,"[9] and "pastoral charity is derived chiefly from the Eucharistic sacrifice which is the center and source of the entire life of the priest, so that the priestly soul strives to make its own what is enacted on the altar of sacrifice."[10] Additionally, the Second Vatican Council affirms of priests:

On the level of their own ministry sharing in the unique office of Christ, the mediator (1 Timothy 2:5), they announce to all the word of God. However, it is in the Eucharistic cult or in the Eucharistic assembly of the faithful (*synaxis*) that they exercise in a supreme degree their sacred functions; there, acting in the person of Christ and proclaiming his ministry, they unite the votive offerings of the faithful to the sacrifice of Christ their head, and in the sacrifice of the Mass they make present again and apply, until the coming of the Lord (see 1 Corinthians 11:26), the unique sacrifice of the New Testament, that namely of Christ offering himself once for all a spotless victim to the Father (see Hebrews 9:11–28).[11]

The centrality of the Eucharist in the life of the priest cannot be overstated. A priest is not ordained to be an administrator; laypersons can sometimes be more effective at administration than a priest. A priest is not primarily a minister to the poor and needy; all the faithful are called to such service, and ordained deacons specifically devote themselves to this ministry. Neither is a priest ordained principally to preach the Gospel, since all Christians are entrusted with the non-liturgical proclamation of the Gospel of Jesus Christ through their lives, and ordained deacons are empowered to preach within the liturgy. A priest is ordained principally to celebrate the Mass—the natural habitat for the Eucharist—and to prepare sinners for receiving the Eucharist worthily through celebration of the sacrament of reconciliation. Only a priest can celebrate the Eucharist and reconciliation, and in these two sacraments the most essential aspects of the Christian life are made accessible to the members of the Church.

The most powerful foreshadowing of Jesus Christ's high priesthood can be found in the person of Melchizedek in the book of Genesis. He is a mysterious figure whom Abram encounters prior to the institution of the Levitical priesthood.

> And Melchizedek king of Salem brought out bread and wine; he was priest of God Most High. And he blessed him [Abram] and said,
> "Blessed be Abram by God Most High,
> maker of heaven and earth;
> and blessed be God Most High,
> who has delivered your enemies into your hand!"
> And Abram gave him a tenth of everything.
> (Genesis 14:18–20)

Pope Benedict XVI comments on the connection between the offering of Melchizedek and the future celebration of the Eucharist in the New Testament: "The offering of bread and wine made by Melchizedek in Abraham's time is fulfilled in the Eucharistic action of Jesus who offers himself in the bread and in the wine and, having conquered death, brings life to all believers."[12] Further, he says:

> In what sense, therefore, was Jesus a priest? The Eucharist itself tells us. We can start with the simple words that describe Melchizedek: He "brought out bread and wine" (Genesis 14:18). This is what Jesus did at the Last Supper: he offered bread and wine and in that action recapitulated the whole of himself and his whole mission. That gesture, the prayer that preceded it and the words with which he accompanied it, contain the full meaning of the mystery of Christ....[13]

The fact that Melchizedek was indeed a foreshadowing of Christ is confirmed at length in the seventh chapter of the Letter to the Hebrews. Sheen comments, "The priesthood of Melchizedek, as symbolic of that of Christ, is eternal.... The 'greatness' of Melchizedek was a foretelling of the greatness of Christ."[14]

THE FEMININE QUESTION

The Church has always taught, "'Only a baptized man...validly receives sacred ordination.'...[T]he ordination of women is not possible" (CCC 1577, quoting Canon 1024).[15] When disputes arose about this teaching during the pontificate of Pope John Paul II, he issued an apostolic letter dedicated to the issue, firmly declaring:

> Wherefore, in order that all doubt may be removed regarding a matter of great importance, a matter which pertains to the Church's divine constitution itself, in virtue of my ministry of confirming the brethren (see Luke 22:32), I declare that the Church has no authority whatsoever to confer priestly ordination on women and that this judgment is to be definitively held by all the Church's faithful.[16]

The Congregation for the Doctrine of the Faith, led by then-Cardinal Joseph Ratzinger, offered the following interpretation:

> This teaching requires definitive assent, since, founded on the written Word of God, and from the beginning constantly preserved and applied in the Tradition of the Church, it has been set forth infallibly by the ordinary and universal Magisterium (see *Lumen Gentium* 25, 2).[17]

Some of the reasons for the prohibition of women priests include the following: (1) Never did the Catholic Church in either the East or the West ordain women to be priests. (2) Jesus himself chose twelve men as his apostles. (3) Although women held important positions in the early Church, the practice of the apostles themselves demonstrates that women were never ordained, not even the most perfect woman to ever live—Mary, the Mother of Jesus!

The issue cannot be reduced to one of equal rights between men and women, since "no one has a *right* to receive the sacrament of Holy Orders" (CCC 1578, emphasis in original). Archbishop Sheen recognizes as counterproductive the overzealous and misguided desire for equality between men and women. He writes, "Modern woman has been made equal with man, but she has not been made happy. She has been 'emancipated,' like a pendulum removed from a clock and now no longer free to swing."[18]

Affirming that men and women have the same nature, dignity, liberties, and ultimate goal of sanctification, Sheen points out— and our everyday experience verifies—that nevertheless they are quite different.

> It is clear that *equity* rather than *equality* should be the basis of all the feminine claims. Equity goes beyond equality by claiming superiority in certain aspects of life. Equity is the perfection of equality, not its substitute. It has the advantages of recognizing the specific difference between man and woman, which equality does not have. As a matter of fact, men and women are not equal in sex; they are quite unequal, and it is only because they are unequal that they complement one another.[19]

Everything stated thus far about the prohibition of women's ordination can be summarized in one point: Women are unable to be ordained because Jesus Christ did not allow it, and the Church has no power other than the power its Lord and Savior has entrusted to it. Consequently, the Catholic Church will never allow women to be ordained to the priesthood.

And yet the feminine dimension of the priesthood is not absent, because at the heart of every holy priest is a deep and authentic Marian spirituality. "Every priest has two mothers: one in the flesh, the other in the spirit," Sheen points out.[20] He beautifully reflects on the gift of the Eucharist as the common bond between Mary and the priesthood, evoking the liturgical symbols of the paten, which holds the Body of Christ, and the chalice, which contains the Blood of Christ. "When her Son was taken down from the Cross and laid in her arms as a paten and drained chalice, she could say the words of consecration as no priest can say them: 'This is my Body; This is my Blood.'"[21] Indeed, "Mary, thou art the Sacristan of the High Priest!"[22]

PUT ON CHRIST

Archbishop Sheen was well aware of the sacrificial dimension of the sacred priesthood. Reflecting on the priest shortage—which was much less a crisis in Sheen's day than it is in our own—he asks, "Could it be that one reason for the fewness of vocations is our failure to stress sacrifice?"[23] In a world dominated by moral indifference, consumerism, and relativism, Sheen reminds us that "the search for vocations begins on our knees."[24]

One specific problem that Sheen noted even in his day is the unwillingness to be recognized as a priest or a religious in public.

Creeping into the Church is this new diabolic super-egotism which betrays a shame of being Christ's. "If I dressed like a priest or a nun, or accepted the authority of the Church when it is opposed to the world, I would be *divisive.*" This is precisely the point: *we were meant* to be *divisive....*[25]

The clerical dress or the religious habit do not make the priest or the nun, anymore than water makes Baptism, or bread the Eucharist or oil Holy Orders, but they are pretty good signs of the mystery they signify. It may be objected that a habit or a collar separate us from the world. Marvelous! We were meant to be a "sign of contra-diction," a people apart.[26]

Sheen recalls an exchange he had with a Jewish man who grasped the importance of "putting on Christ" far better than many Catholics:

I received a call from a Jewish art dealer who inquired if I would be interested in a hundred silver crucifixes. When I visited his shop, he told me he bought them from a commu-nity of nuns who decided not to wear a crucifix. "What's wrong with your Church?"...Some time later I received him into the Church, as on his deathbed he embraced the Crucifix which the Religious had abandoned.[27]

And what about those few priests who fail to live out their voca-tion in holiness and fidelity? The failure of such priests is no surprise to our Lord, who called Judas with full knowledge of the man's future betrayal. Since it is Jesus himself who is the minister of each sacrament in and through the person of the priest, the lack of holiness of a particular priest has no bearing on the efficacy of the sacrament. Perhaps Archbishop Sheen says it best with his quip regarding unworthy priests: "The Lord came into Jerusalem on an ass and He can do it again."[28]

There is hope for the wayward, just as there was hope for Peter after he betrayed Jesus. "Every bad priest is close to being a good one; every good priest is in danger of being a bad one. The line between sanctity and sin is a fine one."[29]

In summary, the heart and soul of the ministerial priesthood consist in the celebration of the Eucharistic sacrifice, and from this central event come the graces needed to fulfill all the duties of priestly ministry. The reservation of priestly ordination to men is by the will of God, and therefore, not even the Church has the power to change this practice.

Just as Jesus Christ was both priest and victim, so too are all priests called to be victims of love for Christ, his Church, and all of his teachings. One powerful and effective way for a priest to witness the love of Christ to a hostile world in a spirit of sacrifice is to wear publicly a Roman collar or religious habit as a sign of his inner consecration to Christ. The solution to the shortage of priests will be found in a renewed spirit of prayer and faithful witness to the cross of Jesus Christ, the "sign of contradiction" to our modern world.

POINTS TO PONDER

- Is there a particular priest who left a lasting, positive impression on you during some period of your life? Who was he, and why was his example so memorable?
- Do you encourage young men to consider a possible vocation to the priesthood?

- How can you help people understand that the small number of immoral priests in our society do not reflect the Church but rather constitute an aberration of the Church's true identity?
- How can you show support for your local priests?
- What indispensable roles do you see women playing in the Church and the pastoral apostolate?

CHAPTER SEVEN

The Pope

I might say, therefore, we will go on "by hook and by crook," and the hook will be the hook of the fisherman, and the crook will be the crook of the shepherd; and with the hook we will catch souls for Christ, and with the crook we will keep them, even to the end of time.[1]

—Fulton Sheen, *The Divine Romance*

Sheen fondly recalls a story about the recently canonized Pope St. John XXIII, a serious shepherd of souls who nonetheless had a knack for subtle wit:

When he was Patriarch of Venice, a high tide flooded the Piazza di San Marco; to escape the rising waters he went into a small wineshop. The man behind the counter recognized him and stammered out, "Dry throat, Eminence?" He shook his head and said, "No, wet feet."[2]

After his election to the papacy, Pope John XXIII received Sheen in an audience. He told the archbishop, "The good Lord knew from all eternity that I would be Pope. He also had eighty years of my lifetime to prepare me. Wouldn't you think that with all that time He would have made me more photogenic."[3] It was one of those rare encounters in which Sheen's own wit would not have the upper hand.

HOLY FATHER

One of the most significant differences between Catholicism and other forms of Christianity is our understanding of the papacy. For many Christians, the concept of a pope vested with the authority of Jesus, and the continuation of that primacy throughout the ages, is considered an invention of early Christians. They see no solid biblical foundations for the papacy. Sheen offers many insights that are helpful in understanding the Catholic Church's teaching.

Priests are called "Father" because they transmit spiritual life, just as human fathers transmit biological life. The pope, called the "Holy Father," bears a unique fatherhood. Sheen tells us that "the origin of the word Pope or *Papa* has been said to be an abbreviation of the words *Pater Patrum*, [meaning] Father of Fathers."[4] Sheen elaborates on this unique fatherhood of the pope: "A father is one who gives life. But he, the Vicar of Christ, gives life, gives life to my mind by keeping the faith of Christ, gives life to my soul by communicating the sacraments of Christ, and gives life to my conscience by guarding the law of Christ."[5]

The Church teaches that, by the direct will of God, the apostle Peter was made the visible head of the Church and was entrusted with the authority of God to teach, govern, and sanctify Christ's Church until the Second Coming. Additionally, this divine authority was to be passed down to Peter's legitimate successors through the ages. All the bishops of the Church around the world are united to the original band of apostles ordained by Jesus Christ to the high priesthood of the new covenant. With the pope as their head, they continue to mediate the grace of Christ to us and teach us the Gospel in all its purity.

Quoting the Second Vatican Council, the *Catechism of the Catholic Church* sums up the matter in this way: "For the Roman Pontiff, by reason of his office as Vicar of Christ, and as pastor of the entire Church has full, supreme, and universal power over the whole Church, a power which he can always exercise unhindered" (CCC 882, quoting *Lumen Gentium*, 22).

The Second Vatican Council clarified that whether the pope is intending to teach infallibly or not, all of his teachings in the domain of faith and morals must be adhered to by all Catholics, since his teachings communicate the truth of Christ:

> In matters of faith and morals, the bishops speak in the name of Christ and the faithful are to accept their teaching and adhere to it with a religious assent. This religious submission of mind and will must be shown in a special way to the authentic magisterium of the Roman Pontiff, even when he is not speaking *ex cathedra*; that is, it must be shown in such a way that his supreme magisterium is acknowledged with reverence, the judgments made by him are sincerely adhered to, according to his manifest mind and will. His mind and will in the matter may be known either from the character of the documents, from his frequent repetition of the same doctrine, or from his manner of speaking.[6]

Archbishop Sheen explains the reason for this religious submission of mind and heart: "Christ is God and God is Truth. Therefore, His teaching, whether communicated through His physical body or through His Mystical Body, must be necessarily true, or infallible."[7]

It may seem that Sheen attributes infallibility to all papal teaching, which is not the way the Church understands infallibility. Yet his observations do make a good deal of sense. If a teaching is true, then we ought to believe it, whether or not it has the added flourish of being "infallibly" true. Jesus did not teach that "the *infallible* truth will make you free," but rather, "the truth will make you free" (John 8:32).

PETER'S PLACE

We might ask why Christianity shifted its center from Jerusalem to Rome. After all, Jesus was born in Bethlehem, worked his miracles throughout the Holy Land, and then suffered, died, rose from the dead, ascended into heaven, and sent the Holy Spirit within the environs of Jerusalem. Since the Holy Land in general, and Jerusalem in particular, is viewed as the cradle of Christianity, why did the Church's center move to Rome only a generation after the ascension of our Lord into heaven? What made Rome the "Eternal City"?

Sheen tells us that this transition was not due to political influence nor military might but simply because "a fisherman went to die there."[8] That fisherman was Peter, the chief of the apostles and the first pope. He was martyred on Vatican Hill in Rome, and the center of Christianity was later transferred to Rome.

The privileged place of Peter among the apostles is evident to anyone reading the Scriptures. Sheen reflects, "He is named one hundred and ninety-five times in the Gospels, while all the other Apostles together are mentioned only one hundred and thirty times."[9] The runner-up for mentions is the apostle John, who is only referred to twenty-nine times.[9]

Not only is Peter the most referenced apostle, but he is always named first in any list of the apostles (see Matthew 10:2; Mark 3:16). Peter is the only person in the New Testament who is given a new name (changed from his birth name of Simon; see Matthew 16:18; Mark 3:16).[10] To Peter alone is given the keys of the kingdom of heaven (Matthew 16:19). Peter is given the mandate to strengthen his brethren, the other apostles (Luke 22:32). To Peter alone is given the thrice-repeated summons to feed the Lord's sheep (John 21:15–17).

Peter is identified in Scripture as the "chief" apostle. The adjective *protos*, used in Matthew 10:2 to modify "Peter," is an adjective of degree rather an adverb of time, suggesting "first in rank or importance." After the ascension, it is Peter who decides that another apostle should be chosen to replace Judas (see Acts 1:15–22). It is Peter who speaks on behalf of the apostles on Pentecost (Acts 2:14–36).

Sheen focuses on an interesting aspect of Peter's life in the early Church. He does not look so much at the things Peter did well or the awesomeness of his office. Rather, he points to his failures. Sheen calls this man "the most human of all humans in the Gospels."[11]

For example, Peter was harshly rebuked by our Lord for attempting to have a savior without a cross (see Matthew 16:21–23). Peter was among the inner band of three who fell asleep while Jesus underwent his agony in the garden (see Matthew 26:40). Peter impetuously resorted to violence when Jesus was arrested, cutting off the ear of one of the servants of the high priest (see John 18:10–11). Most startlingly of all, Peter denied Jesus three times as he warmed himself by a fire while Jesus underwent his harsh interrogation (Matthew 26:69–75; Mark 14:66–72; Luke 22:56–62; John 18:25–27). Sheen reflects, "Never before was any man so cold before a fire!"[12]

In light of these major failures, surely one would think that there were better candidates for the first leader of the Church. "And yet the Son of God chose Peter, who knew sin," Sheen observes, "as the Rock upon which to build His Church, that sinners and the weak might never have excuse to despair."[13] Putting it another way, "And so he who knew by experience the mercy and forgiveness of Our Lord was chosen the head of the Church, in order that the Church might forever practice mercy and kindness."[15]

Peter is able to relate to fellow sinners with mercy and compassion and to encourage them to embrace true conversion of heart. "Tradition has it that Peter wept so much for his sins that his cheeks were furrowed with their penitential streams."[16] Indeed, there is a crucial difference between the remorse of Judas after his betrayal of Jesus and the contrition of Peter after he denied him: "Both did deny the Master and both repented or were sorry. But the Greek word used in the Scripture is not the same in both instances. Judas repented unto himself—he had self-pity. Peter repented unto the Lord—he had penitence, sorrow and a desire for amendment."[17]

After the death of Jesus, Peter continued to show forth his weak humanity. Although Jesus promised his followers that he would indeed rise from the dead on the third day, Peter was prepared to throw in the towel and go back to his old way of life. "I am going fishing," he said to the other apostles (John 21:3). Sheen comments: "The word Peter used implied a progressive or habitually repeated action. Was Peter telling them that he was going permanently to his fishing business? It seems hard to imagine, and yet it is implied in the tense."[18] This is the same Peter who was identified by Jesus as the "Rock" upon which his Church would be built and who was privileged to witness the magnificent Transfiguration shortly before the death of Jesus (see Matthew 16:18; 17:1–6; Mark 9:2–13)!

When the risen Lord appeared to Peter and the others by the sea, Jesus asked Peter if he loved him with a sacrificial love. Peter's response was one of mere friendship, a distinction not noticeable in English but present in the original Greek (see John 21:15–17). "The Lord asked for a love of devotion, and all He got was a love of emotion. But even that He does not reject. It is not enough, He says, but it is enough to start."[19]

This look at Peter's personality and his mission as the first pope of the Church sheds abundant light on the nature of the papacy throughout all of time. Christ's divine plan is clear: "*The way He chose to prolong His teaching is the same as that which He chose to communicate it originally, namely, through human nature.*"[20]

EARTHEN VESSELS

The Church is not without her detractors. Sheen observes, "The enemies of the Papacy failed to make a distinction between *infallibility* and *impeccability*."[21] In the eyes of some persons, holiness is an almost "magical" necessity to authenticate a pope's divine mission. But as we have already seen with Peter, the ability to teach infallibly the faith of Christ, without compromise, has no direct relation to the holiness of the man who is pope.

As Sheen puts it, "If the Church were as good and perfect as some of the critics want it to be, there would be no room for them or us."[22] It is indeed a wonderful consolation for us sinners that "the Church no more expected to have perfect Catholics than our Lord expected to have perfect apostles."[23] We are all works in progress.

Living in the twenty-first century, we give thanks to God for the wonderful popes he has sent to us in recent history. We think of Pope Francis, a pope for the poor and with the poor; Pope Benedict, the servant of the servants of God who humbly resigned from office for the greater good of the Church; Pope St. John Paul II, who formed the "John Paul II generation" and was recently elevated to the glories of the altar. Perhaps one of the most moving photographs of Fulton Sheen was taken on October 2, 1979, only two months before his death. The photo captures Sheen being lovingly embraced by Pope John Paul II, of whom Sheen wrote: "I believe that John Paul II will go down in history as one of the great Pontiffs of all times."[24]

Two popes of the last century risked their lives to protect the innocent in Warsaw and Germany from the aggression of the Soviet Red Army following the First World War. These men were Achille Ratti, at the time a diplomat in Warsaw, and Eugenio Pacelli, who was papal nuncio to Germany.[25] They went on to become Pope Pius XI and Pope Pius XII, respectively.

We also thank God for the popes who served at the very beginning of Christianity. Archbishop Sheen reminds us that of the first thirty-three popes in the history of the Church, thirty of them were killed for their faith, while the other three were exiled.[26]

Indeed, there have been some wicked popes in the history of the Church. However, they were the exception to the rule, and even in their degenerate spiritual states, they publicly preached and taught the true faith of Christ to the masses. Just as Jesus was able to use

Peter's weak, temperamental, and sometimes confused humanity to lead the Church, so too does God in every age continue to write straight with crooked lines.

As Catholics, we are called to share Archbishop Sheen's love and respect for the Holy Father. Sheen's comment about the relationship of bishops to the pope is equally instructive for the lay faithful: "I think bishops are strong *only* when they are united with the Holy Father."[27]

In summary, the historical and biblical foundations of the papacy are evident to anyone who takes the time to examine them. The papacy is not a human invention but a divinely willed institution established for the purpose of leading, sanctifying, and teaching the faithful of Christ's Church. We owe obedience to the Holy Father, and we should pray for him daily as he carries out Christ's mandate of feeding his sheep.

POINTS TO PONDER

- Do you pray for the pope? Do you encourage others to do so?
- Do you have a favorite pope? Who is it, and why is he your favorite?
- What role does the Holy Spirit have in the election of a pope? What role does the College of Cardinals have?
- What do you think is the greatest accomplishment of our current pope?

CHAPTER EIGHT

Mary, the Mother of Jesus

A Catholic boy from a parochial school was telling a university professor who lived next door about the Blessed Mother. The professor scoffed at the boy, saying: "But there is no difference between her and my mother." The boy answered: "That's what you say, but there's a heck of a lot of difference between the sons." [1]

—Fulton Sheen, *The World's First Love*

Fulton Sheen's devotion to the Blessed Virgin Mary planted its roots while Sheen was still an infant. In his autobiography, he fondly shares the fact that when he was baptized, his mother laid him on the altar of the Virgin Mary and consecrated him to her. Sheen reflected, "As an infant may be unconscious of a birthmark, so I was unconscious of the dedication—but the mark was always there. Like a piece of iron to the magnet, I was drawn to her before I knew her, but never drawn to her without Christ." [2]

In the last twenty years of his life, Sheen began to pray that he would die either on a Saturday, devoted to Mary, or on one of her feast days. [3] When his death came on Sunday, December 9, 1979, it seemed that his request was unanswered. Why did he not die the day before on a Saturday that was the Solemnity of the Immaculate Conception of Mary?

Yet a case can be made that God indeed granted Sheen his request. For December 9 is the feast day of St. Juan Diego.

St. Juan Diego, the first indigenous American saint, was like Sheen in many ways. Both were known for their Eucharistic devotion; they were both instrumental in the advancement of evangelization; and both had a great devotion to Our Lady. St. Juan Diego was the visionary of Our Lady of Guadalupe, who is patroness of the Americas. In fact, December 9 commemorates the first apparition of the Blessed Mother to him in 1531. Therefore Sheen did die on a day of great Marian importance, particularly to North America and its evangelization.

Catholic Christianity gives to Mary the highest form of reverence given to a created being, a veneration called *hyperdulia*. In this chapter, we consider Sheen's devotion to Mary and his encouragement to all Catholics to share his filial love for her.

MOTHER AND SON

Modern anti-Marian spirituality is awkward, to say the least. Sheen writes:

> I think one of the major defects in world religions has been the absence of the feminine. The absence becomes more striking in a study of Christian sects where so little attention is paid to the Mother of Christ. It would be strange to visit a friend's home and yet never hear him speak of his mother.[4]

Unfortunately, the inheritors of Protestantism have driven a wedge between Jesus and Mary, as one way among others to demonstrate the differences between Catholic Christianity and non-Catholic Christianity. Of this artificial and revolutionary division, Sheen comments, "It is impossible to love Christ adequately without also loving the Mother who gave Him to us. Those who begin by ignoring her soon end by ignoring Him, for the two are insepa-rable in the great drama of redemption."[5]

Stating the matter more directly, "Mary does not prevent our honoring Our Lord. Nothing is more cruel than to say that she takes souls away from Christ. That could mean that Our Lord chose a mother who is selfish, He Who is love Itself."[6] It would be absurd to separate Mary from her divine son, Sheen says: "Just as you cannot go to a statue of a mother holding a babe, and cut away the mother, leaving the babe suspended in mid-air, neither can you cleave away the Mother from the Babe of Bethlehem."[7]

Why do Catholics venerate Mary? The Second Vatican Council offers the following observation:

> Embracing God's salvific will with a full heart and impeded by no sin, she devoted herself totally as a handmaid of the Lord to the person and work of her Son, under Him and with Him, by the grace of almighty God, serving the mystery of redemption. Rightly therefore the holy Fathers see her as used by God not merely in a passive way, but as freely cooperating in the work of human salvation through faith and obedience.[8]

Sheen looks at the matter this way: "Can you not see that if Christ Himself willed to be physically formed in her for nine months and then be spiritually formed by her for thirty years, it is to her that we must go to learn how to have Christ formed in us? Only she who raised Christ can raise a Christian."[9]

Thus the fact that God chose Mary from all eternity to bear the incarnate Second Person of the Trinity as the *Theotokos* is in itself sufficient reason for us to acknowledge her singular greatness among all created beings. But Mary's greatness transcends *what she did* in bearing the Son of God. It extends to the core of her being, *who she is,* the only perfect woman in the history of humanity.

Sheen asserts,

> God has to have two pictures of us: one is what we *are,* and the other is *what we ought to be.*
>
> ...There is, actually, only one person in all humanity of whom God has one picture and in whom there is a perfect conformity between what He wanted her to be and what she is, and that is His Own Mother.[10]

For those who may recoil at the notion of a perfect created being, Sheen asks, "Do you not think that the Son of God who hates sin would have made His own mother sinless, and He who hates moral ugliness, would have made her immaculately beautiful?"[11] In his classic, down-to-earth style, Sheen explains Mary's perfection: "If you could have preexisted your mother...would you not have made her the most perfect woman that ever lived?... Why, then, should we think that God would do otherwise?"[12]

Sheen reminds us that the first woman, Eve, was also created in a perfect state, and "certainly what God gave to Eve, He would not refuse to His Own Mother."[13] Further linking Eve and Mary, Sheen writes, "As Eden was the Paradise of Creation, Mary is the Paradise of the Incarnation, and in her as a Garden were celebrated the first nuptials of God and man."[14] These "first nuptials" were at the moment she freely said yes to God's invitation to be the Mother of His Son.

SINLESS VIRGIN MOTHER

The fact that Mary was free from all sin, both original sin and personal sin, throughout her lifetime is known as the dogma of the Immaculate Conception. The Church affirms that all human persons, including Mary, are in need of redemption. However, as a singular privilege in light of her vocation to be the Mother of God, the fruits of Christ's redemption were applied to her at the moment of her conception. Thus the dogma of the Immaculate Conception does not detract from Christ nor imply that Mary did not need to be redeemed. It shows forth the power of God working within Mary's free choice always to do his will.

Another important dimension of a proper understanding of Mary is her perpetual virginity in conjunction with her divine maternity. Sheen writes, "If God in His wisdom chose, in one woman, to unite virginity and motherhood, it must be that one is destined to illumine the other."[15] Elaborating on this statement, he indicates:

> Virginity alone lacks something: there is an incomplete-ness about it; something unfulfilled.... Motherhood alone loses something: there is a surrender, an unflow-ering.... Oh! For a *rapprochement* in which there would be a virginity that never lacked anything, and a mother-hood that never lost anything! We have both in Mary, the Virgin Mother.[16]

The modern world, which sometimes views pregnancy as a disease, can learn volumes about the sacredness of motherhood from

Mary. And to this society that idolizes sex and views virginity as a defect, the example of Mary's virginal purity can be profound. She offers a solution to the widespread bankruptcy of morals and brokenness of spirit that ail the contemporary person.

Some Christians object to Mary's perpetual virginity based on Scripture's mention of the "brothers and sisters of the Lord" (see Mark 3:31; 6:3; 1 Corinthians 9:5; Galatians 1:19). The *Catechism* responds:

> The Church has always understood these passages as not referring to other children of the Virgin Mary. In fact James and Joseph, "brothers of Jesus," are the sons of another Mary, a disciple of Christ, whom St. Matthew significantly calls "the other Mary." They are close relations of Jesus, according to an Old Testament expression. (CCC 500, citing Matthew 13:55; 28:1; 27:56; Genesis 13:8; 14:16; 29:15)

One may wonder why Mary's virginity is even relevant. After all, the Church has canonized wives and mothers, so why is it significant that Mary never had sexual intercourse?

A primary reason is that Mary's virginity attests to the intensity of her love for God. It was a love so total and pure that she could not share her body, the tabernacle of the Most High, with any other person. Sheen writes, "She fell in love at a very early age, and it was with God—one of those beautiful loves where the first love is the last love, and the last love is Eternal Love."[17]

Truly, "no other human being ever loved Jesus as much as Mary did," not only because she was the mother who gave him flesh and blood but also because she was unaffected by original sin.[18]

"Of every other child that is born into the world, friends can say that it resembles his mother. This was the first instance in time that anyone could say that the mother resembled the Child."[19]

MEDIATRIX OF GRACE

In addition to offering these insights into the importance of Mary in salvation history, Sheen also addresses her role as mediatrix of grace. The graces Jesus won for us through his cross are distributed to the human race by Christ through Mary. Sheen explains: *"Her Divine Son willed that since she was the nurse and Mother of the Physical Body with which He redeemed the world, so she should be left behind to be the nurse and mother of His Mystical Body...."*[20]

This motherhood would come only after Mary's unfathomable labor pains at the foot of the cross, the peak of the spiritual and emotional pains she suffered from the moment of the presentation of the infant Jesus in the temple.

> From the moment she heard Simeon's words, she would never again lift the Child's hands without seeing a shadow of nails on them; every sunset would be a blood-red image of His Passion.... Every pulse that she would feel in the tiny wrist would be like the echo of an oncoming hammer. If He was dedicated to salvation through suffering, so was she.[21]

Mary is the New Eve and mother of all believers in the order of grace. Sheen said, "The infant Church had need of a mother, just as the infant Christ. She had to remain on earth until her [spiritual] family had grown."[22]

It was on Calvary that Mary became the mother of all Christians. Sheen writes, "The Evangelist who was at the Cross tells us that she stood [at the Cross]. If Eve stood at the foot of the tree, she, the New Eve, would stand at the foot of the Cross—gazing upon a Crucifix."[23]

And after Jesus died, when his body was laid on Mary's lap (so powerfully captured by Michelangelo in his *Pietà*), "it seemed to her that Bethlehem had come back again—but really it had not. Between Bethlehem and Calvary our sins had intervened."[24]

Mary suffered the greatest loss ever known to humanity. Sheen reflects on her emptiness: "She understands sorrows because she lost more than any one else. Some have lost a mother; others a son; others a spouse; but Mary lost everything, for she lost God."[25] Elsewhere he says, "It is hard to lose a son or daughter, but it is harder to bury Christ. To be motherless is a tragedy, but to be Christless is hell."[26]

And yet, in the midst of the greatest sorrow known to the world, Mary displays a profound beauty. Sheen artfully relates Mary's seven sorrows to the Holy Sacrifice of the Mass:

> Mary, Mother of sorrows, Thy seven dolors are like a Holy Mass. In Thy first dolor, thou wert appointed Sacristan by Simeon to keep the Host until the Hour of sacrifice; in Thy second dolor, Thou didst leave the Sacristy to serve the altar as Thy Son's visit sanctified Egypt; in the third dolor, Thou didst recite the Confiteor at the foot of the altar as Thy Son recited His Confiteor to the Doctors of the Law; Thy fourth Dolor was the Offertory as Thou didst make the oblation of His Body and Blood on the way to Calvary; Thy fifth dolor was the Consecration in which Thou didst offer Thine own body and blood in

union with Thy Son's for the Redemption of the world; Thy sixth dolor was the Communion when Thou didst receive the body of Thy Son from the altar of the Cross; and Thy seventh dolor was the *Ite Missa Est* as Thou didst end Thy sorrow with an adieu to the tomb.[27]

It may seem ironic to uphold as a model of hope a seemingly vanquished man and a woman overcome with grief. Sheen suggests a very interesting foreshadowing of this in the two famous epics of Homer, the *Iliad* and the *Odyssey*, with attention to Hector as the defeated hero and Penelope as the sorrowful woman: "For a thousand years before the birth of Our Blessed Lord, pagan antiquity resounded with these two stories of the poet who threw into the teeth of history the mysterious challenge of glorifying a defeated man and hailing a sorrowful woman."[28] Sheen suggests that perhaps God was preparing the pagan world for what would be accomplished by Christ in union with his mother.

As Mediatrix of Grace in virtue of her active cooperation with the life, passion, and death of her Son, Mary is a powerful intercessor on our behalf. Sheen humorously illustrated this through one of his many stories.

One day Our Blessed Lord was walking through the Kingdom of Heaven and saw some souls who had got in very easily. Approaching Peter at the Golden Gate He said: "...You must use your power wisely and discreetly. Tell me, Peter, how did these souls gain entry into My Kingdom?" To which Peter answered: "Don't blame me, Lord. Every time I close the door, Your Mother opens a window."[29]

MODEL FOR HUMANITY

What can we learn from Mary's example? Most importantly, we need to realize that "the main ministry of Mary is to incline men's hearts to obedience to the will of her Divine Son."[30] There is never any competition between authentic Marian spirituality and orthodox Christianity. Of Mary's last recorded words in Scripture, spoken at the wedding of Cana, Sheen writes, "They are the most magnificent words that ever came from the lips of a woman: 'Whatsoever He shall say to you, do ye.'"[31] These are Mary's words to every generation of believers.

We also can learn from Mary the inescapability of suffering. She teaches us to accept our trials in life and offer them up to the Lord: "If the Father gave His Son a Cross and the Mother a sword, then somehow sorrow does fit into the Divine plan of life."[32]

In summary, the reasons for Sheen's veneration of Mary are the same reasons why we should also embrace a healthy Marian spirituality. Mary's privileged position in salvation history includes her divine maternity as the *Theotokos*, as well as the fact that she is the Immaculate Conception and virgin Mediatrix of Grace. Authentic Marian devotion is part of God's plan, and for those who question it, Sheen points out, "Let those who think that the Church pays too much attention to Mary give heed to the fact that Our Blessed Lord Himself gave ten times as much of His life to her as He gave to His Apostles."[33]

Just as one of the best ways we can compliment an artist is to praise his artwork, so too a powerful way of glorifying God is to commend him on his masterpiece. Let us honor Mary and ask for her intercession.

Warning of what may happen if we do not rediscover the importance of Mary in God's plan of salvation history, Sheen writes, "There is a grave danger that, lest in celebrating Christmas without the Mother, we may soon reach a point where we will celebrate Christmas without the Babe.... Just as there can never be a Christmas without a Christ, so there can never be Christ without a Mary."[34]

May Sheen's insights help all of us rediscover she who truly is "our tainted nature's solitary boast."[35]

POINTS TO PONDER

- What is your favorite Marian devotion or prayer? Why?
- How do you respond to someone who claims that Marian spirituality detracts from Christ?
- Mary was the most perfect human person ever to exist, as well as the Mother of God. Looking back to our previous chapter, why was she not a priest? How does this relate to Church ministry today?
- Which quality or qualities of Mary appeal to you the most? How can you follow her example in daily life?
- Pope St. John Paul II described the rosary as "a Christocentric prayer."[36] What do you think he meant by this? Has this prayer drawn you closer to the Lord?

Contraception and Abortion

Just think what a havoc would have been wrought among the birth-control propagandists if the mothers of those who preached it had practiced it![1]

—Fulton Sheen, *Old Errors and New Labels*

Reflecting on the role of children in family life, Sheen recalls the observation of an ancient Greek historian:

Plutarch tells us that one day Julius Caesar saw some wealthy foreign women in Rome carrying dogs in their arms, and he said: "Do the women in their country never bear children?" Apparently, even in those days, maternal instincts which should have been directed to children were perverted, in certain cases, to pomeranians.[2]

For many people, the topics of birth control and abortion are highly personal and private. Discussions about these issues with a mixed crowd can become tense and frustrating. Yet the fact is that the Gospel message has great bearing on human sexuality and its relationship to new life. Christ's call to communion is an invitation to the whole person, and one vital dimension of our personhood is our sexuality.

In this chapter, we will explore Fulton Sheen's outlook on contraception and abortion. His perspective will help us better understand God's timeless and eternal law, a law that is directed to our authentic happiness.

CONTRACEPTION

Contraception may broadly refer to anything that has as its purpose the prevention of conception—hence the name "contraception," meaning "against conception." Most people know that the Church teaches that sexual relations are only to be exercised between married persons, so the next related question that is generally asked is: What does the Church say about the use of contraceptives between married persons? Since married persons are allowed to have sexual intercourse, what is the big deal about whether they choose to use contraception?

Few people realize that Christianity as a whole banned contraception for the first nineteen centuries. Contraception was clearly recognized as an evil, because "planned unparenthood is the deliberate and willful decision on the part of a husband and wife to exclude from God the opportunity to create another to His image and likeness."[3] It was not until 1930 that the Anglicans became the first Christian group to buckle under the pressure of a permissive culture and allow contraception. This landmark decision found widespread acceptance among the various and multiple Protestant denominations. Less than a year later, virtually every Christian denomination of the Federal Council of Churches had voiced agreement with the Anglican position.

One formidable exception remained: the Catholic Church, which firmly believes that "right is still right if nobody is right, and wrong is still wrong if everybody is wrong."[4] Perhaps the clearest teaching of the Church against contraception and abortion may be found in Pope Paul VI's encyclical *Humanae Vitae*:

> The direct interruption of the generative process already begun and, above all, all direct abortion, even for therapeutic reasons, are to be absolutely excluded as lawful means of regulating the number of children. Equally to be condemned, as the magisterium of the Church has affirmed on many occasions, is direct sterilization....[5]

This teaching of the Church has been constant, and it is unchangeable, since it simply states with clarity the teaching that Almighty God has inscribed in the order of creation. Sheen points out that "it is too often said that birth-control is wrong because the Catholic Church says it is wrong. No, birth-control is wrong because reason says it is wrong; it is the misuse and abuse of certain faculties that God has given to mankind."[6]

Artificial birth control, which "assists in neither birth nor control,"[7] violates the very purpose for which God gave us our sexual faculties. It sends to God a message that he was mistaken, that he did not know what he was doing when he created us as fecund, sexual beings.

Sheen reminds us that we do not need religion to convince us that birth control is unnatural and wrong; sound philosophy and proper thinking are all that is needed. The prohibition of contraception is grounded in God's all-wise ordering of the universe, and it is discernible through reason. The Catholic Church does not have the authority to overrule this prohibition or even to offer a compromise. The sooner opponents of the Church's teaching recognize this fact, the sooner more fruitful discussion can be held among those who sincerely seek to understand the Catholic perspective.

GOD IS LOVE

How does contraception oppose God's plan for humanity?

Sheen points out that God is love, and the nature of love is to be diffusive. Love expands and envelops all who surrender to it. Sheen writes, "Sterile, selfish love is the negation of love. A love that refuses to propagate itself is not love."[8]

This is to say that couples who use contraception express the body language proper to love, but in reality their minds and hearts are far from it. An act intended by God to be an outward expression of marital love becomes a lie. It falsifies what Pope St. John Paul II calls the "language of the body."

> When the conjugal act is *deprived of its inner truth* because it is deprived artificially of its procreative capacity, it also *ceases to be an act of love.* One can say that in the case of an artificial separation of these two meanings [procreation and union] in the conjugal act, a real bodily union is brought about, but it does not correspond to the inner truth and dignity of personal communion, "*communio personarum.*" This communion demands, in fact, that the "language of the body" be expressed reciprocally in the integral truth of its meaning. If this truth is lacking, one can speak neither of the truth of the reciprocal gift of self nor of the reciprocal acceptance of oneself by the person. Such a violation of the inner order of conjugal communion, a communion that plunges its roots into the very order of the person, *constitutes the essential evil of the contraceptive act.*[9]

Contraception wrecks family life. In fact, Pope Paul VI warned in his encyclical, released in 1968, of what would happen if contraception became an accepted practice:

> ...Let them first consider how easily this course of action could open wide the way for marital infidelity and a general lowering of moral standards. Not much experience is needed to be fully aware of human weakness and to understand that human beings—and especially the young, who are so exposed to temptation—need incentives to keep the moral law, and it is an evil thing to make it easy for them to break that law. Another effect that gives cause for alarm is that a man who grows accustomed to the use of contraceptive methods may forget the reverence due to a woman, and, disregarding her physical and emotional equilibrium, reduce her to being a mere instrument for the satisfaction of his own desires, no longer considering her as his partner whom he should surround with care and affection.
>
> Finally,... [w]ho will blame a government which in its attempt to resolve the problems affecting an entire country resorts to the same measures as are regarded as lawful by married people in the solution of a particular family difficulty?... Should they regard this as necessary, they may even impose their use on everyone....[10]

These predictions of Pope Paul VI—of increased marital infidelity, a general lowering of moral standards, loss of the personal dignity of spouses, and government-mandated birth-control regulations—have all come to pass. It is surely time for human society to come to its senses and realize that it is bringing about its own destruction.

Sheen recalls the horror of the first "birth-control movement" in the early Church:

> The first direct, human limitation of infant life in the history of Christianity took place in the village of Bethlehem through an infant-controller whose name was Herod. That prevention of infant life was simultaneously an attack upon Divinity in the person of God made man, Jesus Christ, our Lord. No one strikes at birth who does not simultaneously strike at God, for birth is earth's reflection of the Son's eternal generation.[11]

The stark truth is that there is sometimes little difference between Herod's pride and selfishness and the pride and selfishness that fuel the contraceptive industry today. In both cases, the individual claims absolute mastery over the gift of life; in both instances, the laws of God are ignored; and in both instances, the result is misery. Even back in 1951, Sheen commented that "medical opinion today is that the increasing psychoses and neuroses in women are due to a flight from motherhood.... Five out of every six cases of divorce, or 83 1/3 percent, stem from marriages having no children."[12]

Sheen reminds us that "the gravest danger facing modern society, one which has brought the ruin of older civilizations and is destined to effect the collapse of our own unless we prevent it, is the loss of the sense of sin."[13] Through chastity and self-control, we can once again take full possession of ourselves and be a leaven to society. Ours is the authentic happiness of the people of God.

THE BLESSING OF CHILDREN

Children are not merely "products" of marriage, nor are they "tolerable burdens." Rather, they are the crowning jewels of marriage. Church teaching proclaims that children are the "supreme gift of marriage," who "contribute greatly to the good of the parents themselves" (CCC 1652, quoting *Gaudium et Spes*, 50). In fact, the term *matrimony* comes from two Latin words, *matris* and *munus*, meaning "the office of motherhood."

Our Lord manifested the intrinsic value of children during his public ministry (see Mark 10:13–16). Sheen comments, "When the apostles drove away the children, our Lord rebuked them and was much displeased. In fact, the strongest word that could be found in Greek for 'rebuke' is used in the Gospel on this occasion."[14]

Ignoring the privileged place of children in the divine plan has consequences. The practice of contraception turns the drama of life into boredom and self-absorption. The proper understanding of marriage, on the other hand, is truly liberating. Marriage fosters a mature understanding of human sexuality as it "releases the flesh from its individual selfishness for the service of the family."[15]

Sheen refers to the "messianic character" of children within the family: "They represent the conquest of Love over the insatiable ego; they symbolize deceit of selfishness and the victory of charity. Each child begets disinterestedness, inspires a sacrifice."[16]

Staying up all night with a sick child, missing the end-of-the-year party at work in order to attend a child's basketball game, buying your child a new bike instead of getting yourself that new electronic device you have been wanting—these are examples of the small sacrifices we make for our children. Our goal is not only to provide for them, love them, and develop their character but to increase our own virtue as well.

Sometimes parents of large families receive hostile glares from passersby. The inference is that their generosity toward life somehow detracts from couples who choose sterility. Some parents report angry looks even at church when their little ones make the slightest of noises.

How often are priests and deacons tempted to be short-tempered with their young altar servers? Are they also reluctant to preach what Jesus taught on the beauty of fecundity and the evils of contraception? When was the last time you heard a homily that praised large families and decried the evils of contraception and abortion?

The Church does not deny the need for families to sometimes regulate their size. Responsible parenthood calls for self-control, which is a central dimension of Natural Family Planning (known also as NFP). As C.S. Lewis might remark, we are not mere "trousered apes" but beings made in God's image and likeness who have the use of reason.[17]

Unlike animals directed by instincts, human persons act in freedom and therefore with responsibility. Human beings choose when to have sexual relations and when to abstain from them. When it is not in the best interest of the family to bring another child into the world—a determination the couple must make in prayer—spouses refrain from sexual relations during the wife's fertile time of the month. By exercising this self-control and choosing a nonsexual way to communicate their love for each other, husband and wife are able to grow in virtue, respect God's law, and defer the gift of pregnancy. It is a win-win situation for the whole family!

Of course, there is always a danger that even NFP-practicing couples will slip into a contraceptive mentality. They might decide to abstain from sexual relations during the wife's fertile time for arbitrary reasons. Should this happen, they cease to cooperate with God's plan for the transmission of life and enter into the domain of sin. John Paul II stated the matter in this way: "The use of 'infertile periods' in conjugal shared life can become a source of abuses if the couple thereby attempts to evade procreation without just reasons, lowering it below the morally just level of birth in their family."[18]

How do couples know whether their reasons for postponing the possibility of pregnancy are morally acceptable? By asking the following question: With an informed conscience and before God, is postponing the possibility of pregnancy truly in the best interest of our current and future family? Are our motives serious and upright (that is, due to medical, psychological, financial situations, and so on),[19] or are they based on greed and selfishness and a flight from sacrifice? Honest responses to this question throughout married life will serve the couple well.

No one said that God's teaching against contraception would be easy. Sheen comments, "I believe that the [encyclical] *Humanae Vitae* is one of the great tests of the Church in our times."[20] Perhaps one of the reasons why this teaching is difficult is that it calls for restraint and sacrifice with respect to one of the strongest urges of the human person. It calls us to focus not on our own attainment of pleasure and satisfaction but on the good of the spouse, the family, and the potential new life that can come from this union.

ABORTION

Given everything said above about contraception, it should go without saying that the evil of abortion is even greater. Contraception and abortion are more closely linked than one may initially think. A number of contraceptive pills on the market today are not merely intended to prevent conception. Should conception still take place, they have a backup mechanism that will prevent a fertilized egg from implanting in the uterine wall. These forms of contraceptives are known as abortifacients, since they directly cause abortions.

If it appears that Sheen does not address the issue of abortion in his many books, it is because abortion was not yet legal and therefore not common during Sheen's literary years. Yet during the summer of 1976, three years after abortion became legal in the United States with the 1973 *Roe v. Wade* Supreme Court decision, Sheen addressed a crowd in Philadelphia on the issue.

> Notice that the heavenly messenger did not tell Mary that she would conceive a fetus. No! She would conceive and bear a Son, a person, a Child of the Most High God. It was inconceivable to her that because of her poverty, the overpopulation in Bethlehem, inadequate housing and the shame attached to the unusual nature of her conception that she would thwart the life within her, as some women do today. Life is sacred.[21]

Let us remove the issues of abortion and contraception from the realm of political expedience and social permission and see them in the context of human dignity. In the light of God's big picture for humanity, the evil of abortion and contraception is obvious. They are violations of human freedom and of our call to holiness.

Sheen writes, "Perhaps the most materialistic birth-controller in the world would admit bringing a son into the world if she were certain he would become President; why should she scruple at bringing one into the world if she were certain he was to become an adopted son of God?"[22]

In summary, the Church's absolute and unchanging prohibition of contraception and the even greater scourge of abortion is grounded in God's own law and is directed to our own authentic happiness. Children are the greatest blessing of marriage, and the sacrifices that they inspire can contribute wonderfully to the sanctification of their parents. By building a strong culture of life within the home, we model to our children the values that are most important and empower them to make the right decisions on the long but exciting road to holiness.

Points to Ponder

- Do you know and understand the Church's teaching on the regulation of birth? Is there anything holding you back from embracing it?
- If you are among the many who are unable to have children, in what other ways can you bear fruit for God's kingdom?
- What can you do to stop the culture of death in our nation?
- Given that the use of contraceptives blocks the expression of unconditional love, why do you think it continues to be popular in our day?

CHAPTER TEN

Divorce and Remarriage

There once was a time when a man who married a woman would no more have thought of divorcing her than of murdering her. But those were the days when men loved because they believed in God; now they lust because they believe in Freud.[1]

—Fulton Sheen, *The Seven Virtues*

Fulton Sheen tells us a story about the hermit St. Macarius of Egypt, who had a vision of an angel. The angel told the surprised hermit that, although he was advancing in holiness, he still was less holy than two women who lived in a town not far from his hermitage. The angel suggested that the hermit pay a visit to the two women in order to learn the mystery of their holiness. Sheen shares what Macarius learned about these two women, as well as the lesson for us:

> For fifteen years they had been married to two brothers and had lived together under the same roof, never once quarreling nor permitting a single unpleasant word to pass between them. Thus did St. Macarius learn that peaceful cohabitation can be even more praiseworthy in the eyes of God than solitary fasting and prayer.[2]

It is appropriate that this chapter immediately follows the chapter on contraception and abortion. As Sheen observes, "The two most evident symptoms of the breakdown of the family are: divorce and voluntary or deliberate sterility, *i.e.* broken contracts and frustrated loves."[3] Although it is nearly impossible to ascertain the number of divorces among Catholics today, and mindful of the fact that sociological studies tend to be inconsistent, the fact of the matter is that the number has grown significantly over the past several decades. Sheen's reflections on the problem can help us confront this situation today with love and humility.

TILL DEATH DO US PART

An essential characteristic of the divinely instituted sacrament of marriage is its permanence, which is also known as its indissolubility. Jesus reaffirms the indissolubility of marriage, as intended by God from the very beginning:

> "What therefore God has joined together, let no man put asunder." They said to him, "Why then did Moses command one to give a certificate of divorce, and to put her away?" He said to them, "For your hardness of heart Moses allowed you to divorce your wives, but from the beginning it was not so. And I say to you: whoever divorces his wife, except for *porneia*,[4] and marries another, commits adultery." (Matthew 19:6–9)

Two points stand out in this teaching of Jesus. First, marriage is, by its very nature, indissoluble; yet secondly, there are instances in which divorce is permitted but not subsequent remarriage.

The first teaching is the basis for the second. A consummated, sacramental marriage is absolutely indissoluble, so it is not possible to enter into a second marriage while the first spouse is still living. By "consummated, sacramental marriage" is meant a marriage between two baptized Christians who have engaged in non-contraceptive sexual intercourse at any point after their marriage to each other. Because a consummated marriage between baptized Christians participates in the love of Christ for his Church, no power other than death can dissolve the marriage bond (see CCC 1640).

What about annulments? An annulment is a Church declaration that what was thought to be a marriage was not actually a true marriage. Those who receive annulments and get married after the annulment is granted are not technically entering a second marriage, because the first marriage never truly existed.

The only instance of being allowed to enter into a second marriage is when the first marriage bond is dissolved—either through the death of the spouse or through the limited intervention of the Church. In these cases, there is nothing sinful or wrong in remarrying.

The majority of remarriages in our society do not match these scenarios. This brings us to the second teaching Jesus presents: When there is divorce without either a subsequent annulment or a dissolution of the bond, remarriage is never permitted.

The "exception clause" of Matthew 19:9, "except for *porneia*," allows for divorce in some instances but not for subsequent remarriage. This interpretation can also be seen in Matthew 5:32: "But I say to you that every one who divorces his wife, except on the ground of *porneia*, makes her an adulteress; and whoever marries a divorced woman commits adultery." This passage again offers grounds for divorce but not for remarriage.

Why would Jesus allow divorce when it is not part of God's original plan? Sheen helps us understand:

> What if the husband becomes an alcoholic, or unfaithful, or beats his wife and children? What if the wife becomes nagging, or unfaithful, or neglects her children? Should there not be a separation? Yes, under certain circumstances there may be a separation, but this does not give the offended party the right to contract a new marriage.[5]

Because the bond of marriage is indissoluble, it cannot be broken by the sins of the couple, and therefore no remarriage is allowed. Yet for pastoral reasons, the Church does not force married couples to live with one another in the same household if there is violence, infidelity, or other grave circumstances.

A civil divorce does not break the bond of marriage. Only God is the author of marriage. Rightfully unhappy with the permissive attitude toward divorce by civil authorities, Sheen declares, "The State should defend the indissolubility of the marriage ties rather than weaken the sanctity of contracts, for divorces are in the highest degree hostile to the prosperity of families and of States, springing as they do from the depraved morals of the people."[6]

Regardless of what civil courts may judge, the Catholic Church does not recognize the marriage of a Catholic outside of the Church. The *Catechism* addresses the gravity of the situation:

> Today there are numerous Catholics in many countries who have recourse to civil *divorce* and contract new civil unions. In fidelity to the words of Jesus Christ,... the Church maintains that a new union cannot be recognized as valid, if the first marriage was. If the divorced

are remarried civilly, they find themselves in a situation that objectively contravenes God's law. Consequently, they cannot receive Eucharistic communion as long as this situation persists. For the same reason, they cannot exercise certain ecclesial responsibilities. Reconciliation through the sacrament of Penance can be granted only to those who have repented for having violated the sign of the covenant and of fidelity to Christ, and who are committed to living in complete continence. (CCC 1650)

WHY DO PEOPLE DIVORCE?

The question may be asked, what motivates spouses to divorce? There are divorces due to serious hardships imposed by one or both spouses, as noted above. But what about the common cases of divorce for non-serious reasons?

One cause of a desire to leave one's spouse is the mistaken identification of sexual attraction with true love. Sheen observes, "The Church has been dealing with marriage for twenty centuries, and yet nowhere in her marriage ceremony does she speak of sex—but she does speak of love."[7] He points out that "it is because of this failure to distinguish between the glandular and spiritual—or between sex, which we have in common with animals, and love, which we have in common with God—that marriages are so full of deception."[8]

Whereas men and women ought to be drawn to one another by authentic love, recognizing each other as unique persons made in God's image and likeness, all too often they fixate on the sexual good of the other. Sheen identifies this with a Freudian mentality: "Freudianism interprets man in terms of sex; Christianity interprets sex in terms of man."[9] Whereas human sexuality is good and beautiful, it is simply one dimension of the human person.

Sheen reflects, "Our modern world does not really love woman; it loves only her external beauty. If it loved woman, it would love woman as long as she is woman. But because it loves the mask of a woman, it ignores the woman when the mask disappears."[10]

If a man falls in love with a woman's beauty and charm, and not with the woman as a person, then he is setting both of them up for disaster when her beauty and charm diminish over time. Whereas it is normal and healthy for a man to be attracted to a woman's exterior qualities, those qualities are meant to give the man reason to get to know her as a person and to fall in love with her as a person. Sexual attraction can be experienced apart from authentic love. "The greatest illusion of lovers is to believe that the intensity of their sexual attraction is the guarantee of the perpetuity of their love."[11]

Another reason for marital breakup—in fact, the one that Sheen identifies as the most destructive and prevalent—is the refusal of spouses to make sacrifices for one another.[12] This is rooted in a desire for pleasure without its concomitant challenges. Family life can be very demanding and even exhausting at times, and only when we agree to put our own interests and comfort zones aside through sacrifice can we purify our love and grow in virtue and holiness. Sheen observes, "As the violin needs tuning, as a block of marble needs cutting before it can make a statue, so the love of husband and wife needs purification before it can rise to new heights."[13]

Frequently the pain of divorce is followed by a quest for another marriage. But if the problems underlying the divorce were caused by the spouse seeking another marriage, the situation moves from bad to worse. "A search for a new partner begins on the assumption that some other human being can supply what only God can give. The new marriages become only the addition of zeros."[14]

FIGHTING FOR MARRIAGE

What is the solution to the difficulties found in marriage? Sheen responds that "the modern solution in marriage is to find a new love; the Christian solution is to recapture an old love.... The modern solution is to chase new prey; the Christian solution is to bind up the wounds of the Divinely sanctioned marriage."[15]

In other words, the answer is sacrifice. Sheen reminds us that "men only fight for what they love."[16] If they truly love their wives, they should fight to keep the marriage together during difficult times. Sheen describes this type of resolution made by one disenchanted but optimistic wife:

> I was thinking of divorce, but I know that if I divorce him, I am contributing to the ruin of civilization. It does not mean very much if I pull my own individual finger out of the dam; just a little water will come through. But if every woman in the world in a similar situation does the same, then the floodtides will sweep over the world. So I am going to stick it out; but I cannot do so without faith, and you must help me to get it.[17]

It is all the more important that we fight for our marriages in this day and age, since we are living in an era in which religious freedom and family values are challenged more than ever. The floodtides *are* sweeping over the world. Sheen reflects:

> It was not so many years ago that those who rejected many Christian truths were considered off the reservation; e.g.

the divorced who remarried, the atheists, the enemies of the family, or those who held that law was the dictate of the will, not of reason. Today, it is we who are considered off the reservation.[18]

Practically, how can spouses "fight" for their marriage? What are the conditions for a healthy marriage? The teachings of the *Catechism of the Catholic Church* and Pope St. John Paul II are particularly instructive:

> This unequivocal insistence on the indissolubility of the marriage bond may have left some perplexed and could seem to be a demand impossible to realize. However, Jesus has not placed on spouses a burden impossible to bear, or too heavy.... It is by following Christ, renouncing themselves, and taking up their crosses that spouses will be able to "receive" the original meaning of marriage and live it with the help of Christ [see Matthew 19:11]. This grace of Christian marriage is a fruit of Christ's cross, the source of all Christian life. (CCC 1615)

> There is no doubt that these conditions must include persistence and patience, humility and strength of mind, filial trust in God and in His grace, and frequent recourse to prayer and to the sacraments of the Eucharist and of Reconciliation. Thus strengthened, Christian husbands and wives will be able to keep alive their awareness of the unique influence that the grace of the sacrament of marriage has on every aspect of married life, including therefore their sexuality: the gift of the Spirit, accepted and responded to by husband and wife, helps them to live

their human sexuality in accordance with God's plan and as a sign of the unitive and fruitful love of Christ for His Church.[19]

Even to couples in difficult situations—perhaps one spouse is an alcoholic, has been unfaithful, or has fallen into some other serious moral predicament—Sheen offers strong advice on fighting for the marriage:

> *Stick it out!* Remain faithful! Why? Suppose the husband, instead of being an alcoholic, had pneumonia. Would the wife nurse him and care for him? If he is a sinner he has moral pneumonia and is spiritually sick; why abandon him?...St. Paul tells us that "the believing wife sanctifieth the unbelieving husband; the believing husband sanctifieth the unbelieving wife." There can be a transfusion of power from one to the other. Sometimes the condition of making the other better is perseverance and love.[20]

Additionally, it would be in the best interest of political leaders and institutions to end their permissive attitude toward divorce and their efforts to redefine traditional marriage. In 1930 Pope Pius XI observed:

> Experience has taught that unassailable stability in matrimony is a fruitful source of virtuous life and of habits of integrity. Where this order of things obtains, the happiness and well being of the nation is safely guarded; what the families and individuals are, so also is the State, for a body is determined by its parts. Wherefore, both for the private good of husband, wife and children, as likewise for the public good of human society, they indeed deserve

well who strenuously defend the inviolable stability of matrimony.[21]

Taking this relationship between marriage and patriotism a step further, Sheen is convinced that:

> Once a citizenry does not feel bound to the most natural and democratic of all self-governing commonwealths, the home, it will not be long until it ceases to feel bound to a nation. The traitors to the home today are the traitors to the nation tomorrow. A people who are not loyal to a home will not be loyal to a flag.[22]

In summary, the Church's prohibition against divorce and remarriage is grounded in the teachings of God, and therefore it cannot be changed. Every marriage will go through difficult times, and spouses should rise to the occasion and address their problems, rather than flee from them through divorce and subsequent remarriage. Strong, permanent marriages are a source of support and strength for children. The more government supports healthy, traditional families, the more loyal its future generations will be.

Points to Ponder

- Is your marriage "divorce-proof"? What can you do to make your love for your spouse more authentic?
- Is there a married couple who has been a terrific witness to you about married life?
- How can you give engaged couples an accurate view of married life, including its challenges and difficulties?
- How can you reach out to a person who has experienced divorce?

NOTES

INTRODUCTION
1. Fulton J. Sheen, *Missions and the World Crisis* (), p. .

CHAPTER ONE
1. Fulton J. Sheen, *For God and Country* (New York: P.J. Kenedy & Sons, 1941), p. 41.
2. Quoted in Thomas C. Reeves, *America's Bishop: The Life and Times of Fulton J. Sheen* (New York: Encounter, 2001), p. 39.
3. Fulton J. Sheen, *Treasure in Clay: The Autobiography of Fulton J. Sheen* (San Francisco: Ignatius, 1993), p. 12.
4. Sheen, *Treasure in Clay*, p. 12.
5. Fulton J. Sheen, *The Eternal Galilean* (New York: Garden City, 1950), p. 93.
6. Fulton J. Sheen, *The Mystical Body of Christ* (New York: Sheed and Ward, 1935), pp. 308–309.
7. Fulton J. Sheen, *Life Is Worth Living: Second Series* (New York: McGraw-Hill, 1954), pp. 159–160.
8. Fulton J. Sheen, *Old Errors and New Labels* (New York: Garden City, 1950), p. 277.
9. Fulton J. Sheen, *Philosophies at War* (New York: Charles Scribner's Sons, 1943), pp. 68–69.
10. Fulton J. Sheen, *Seven Pillars of Peace* (New York: Charles Scribner's Sons, 1944), pp. 79–80.
11. Fulton J. Sheen, *Moods and Truths* (New York: Garden City, 1950), p. 61.
12. Sheen, *Treasure in Clay*, pp. 300–301.
13. Sheen, *Treasure in Clay*, p. 305.
14. Sheen, *Treasure in Clay*, pp. 172–174.
15. Sheen, *Treasure in Clay*, p. 304.
16. Fulton J. Sheen, *Seven Words to the Cross* (New York: P.J. Kenedy & Sons, 1944), p. 29.
17. Fulton J. Sheen, *Go to Heaven* (London: Catholic Book Club, 1962), p. 77.
18. Fulton J. Sheen, *Guide to Contentment* (New York: Alba, 1996), p. 47.
19. Sheen, *Guide to Contentment*, p. 123.

20. See Sheen, *Treasure in Clay,* p. 52.
21. See Sheen, *Treasure in Clay,* p. 70.
22. See Sheen, *Treasure in Clay,* p. 75.
23. Sheen, *Guide to Contentment,* p. 147.
24. Sheen, *Treasure in Clay,* p. 54.
25. Sheen, *Treasure in Clay,* p. 51.
26. Sheen, *Treasure in Clay,* p. 54.
27. Sheen, *Treasure in Clay,* p. 350.
28. Fulton J. Sheen, *The Cross and the Crisis* (Freeport, N.Y: Books for Libraries, 1969), pp. 142–143.
29. Sheen, *The Cross and the Crisis,* p. 193.
30. Fulton J. Sheen, *The Power of Love* (New York: Image, 1964), p. 95.
31. Sheen, *The Seven Pillars of Peace,* p. 77.
32. *Gravissimum Educationis,* 3.
33. *Familiaris Consortio,* 36.
34. *Familiaris Consortio,* 36.
35. *Gaudium et Spes,* 52.
36. Sheen, *Go to Heaven,* p. 75.
37. Sheen, *Old Errors and New Labels,* p. 105.
38. Sheen, *Moods and Truths,* pp. 164–165.
39. Sheen, *Moods and Truths,* pp. 162, 170.

CHAPTER TWO
1. Sheen, *The Cross and the Crisis,* p. 183.
2. See Sheen, *Treasure in Clay,* p. 17.
3. *Gaudium et Spes,* 10.
4. Sheen, *Moods and Truths,* pp. 19, 22.
5. Sheen, *Old Errors and New Labels,* p. 194.
6. Fulton J. Sheen, *Love One Another* (New York: Garden City, 1953), p. 46.
7. Sheen, *Old Errors and New Labels,* pp. 194–195.
8. Fulton J. Sheen, The *Life of All Living* (New York: Popular Library, 1958), pp. 131–132.
9. Fulton J. Sheen, *The Seven Last Words* (New York: D. Appleton-Century, 1934), p. 17.
10. Fulton J. Sheen, *Religion without God* (New York: Garden City, 1954), p. 82.
11. *Gaudium et Spes,* 19.
12. Sheen, *Old Errors and New Labels,* pp. 87–88.

13. Sheen, *Religion without God*, p. vii.
14. Sheen, *The Eternal Galilean*, p. 129.
15. Sheen, *Old Errors and New Labels*, p. 320.
16. Sheen, *Philosophies at War*, p. 95.
17. Fulton J. Sheen, *The Moral Universe: A Preface to Christian Living* (Milwaukee: Bruce, 1936), pp. 169–170.
18. Fulton J. Sheen, *Those Mysterious Priests* (Garden City, N.Y.: Doubleday, 1974), pp. 205–206.
19. Sheen, *Old Errors and New Labels*, p. 250.
20. Sheen, *Moods and Truths*, p. 76.
21. Sheen, *Moods and Truths*, p. 130.
22. Sheen, *The Seven Last Words*, p. 51.
23. Sheen, *The Mystical Body of Christ*, p. 340.
24. Fulton J. Sheen, *Freedom Under God* (Milwaukee: Bruce, 1940), pp. 5–6.
25. Sheen, *The Moral Universe*, p. 13.
26. *Gaudium et Spes*, 16; see Pius XII, *Radio address on the correct formation of a Christian conscience in the young*, March 23, 1952: AAS (1952), p. 271.
27. Sheen, *The Cross and the Crisis*, p. 199.
28. Sheen, *The Mystical Body of Christ*, pp. 292–293.
29. Sheen, *Life Is Worth Living: Second Series*, p. 212.
30. Sheen, *Philosophies at War*, p. 141.
31. Fulton J. Sheen, *A Declaration of Dependence* (Milwaukee: Bruce, 1941), pp. 123, 95.
32. *Gaudium et Spes*, 22.
33. Sheen, *Old Errors and New Labels*, p. 226.
34. Sheen, *The Cross and the Crisis*, p. 136. Emphasis in original.

CHAPTER THREE
1. Sheen, *The Seven Last Words*, pp. 57–58. Emphasis in original.
2. Reeves, p. 251.
3. Quoted in Reeves, p. 254.
4. Quoted in Reeves, p. 288.
5. Sheen, *Love One Another*, p. 46.
6. Fulton J. Sheen, *These Are the Sacraments* (New York: Hawthorn, 1962), p. 9.
7. Sheen, *Love One Another*, p. 30.
8. Fulton J. Sheen, *The Cross and the Beatitudes* (New York: Garden City, 1952), p. 86.

9. Sheen, *The Eternal Galilean*, p. 213.
10. Fulton J. Sheen, *The Rainbow of Sorrow* (New York: Garden City, 1953), p. 80.
11. Sheen, *The Life of All Living*, p. 90.
12. Sheen, *Treasure in Clay*, p. 99.
13. Pope John Paul II, Apostolic Letter on the Christian Meaning of Human Suffering, *Salvifici Doloris*, 26. Emphasis in original.
14. John Paul II, *Salvifici Doloris*, 18, 19. Emphasis in original.
15. Sheen, *Life Is Worth Living: Second Series*, p. 194.
16. Sheen, *Life Is Worth Living: Second Series*, p. 195.
17. Sheen, *The Seven Last Words*, p. 17.
18. John Paul II, *Salvifici Doloris*, 26. Emphasis in original.
19. Adapted from Fulton J. Sheen, *Calvary and the Mass: A Missal Companion* (New York: Garden City, 1953), p. 35. Emphasis in original.
20. Sheen, *Calvary and the Mass*, p. 38.
21. Sheen, *The Rainbow of Sorrow*, p. 30.
22. John Paul II, *Salvifici Doloris*, 27.
23. Sheen, *Seven Words to the Cross*, p. 17.
24. Fulton J. Sheen, *Seven Words of Jesus and Mary* (New York: Garden City, 1953), p. 28.
25. See Fulton J. Sheen, *The World's First Love* (San Francisco: Ignatius, 1996), p. 258.
26. Fulton J. Sheen, *Life Is Worth Living: Fourth Series* (New York: McGraw-Hill, 1956), p. 240.
27. John Paul II, *Salvifici Doloris*, 24. Emphasis in original.
28. Sheen, *The Mystical Body of Christ*, pp. 300–301.
29. John Paul II, *Salvifici Doloris*, 19. Emphasis in original.
30. Fulton J. Sheen, *The Way of the Cross* (Huntington, Ind.: Our Sunday Visitor, 1982), p. 12.
31. Sheen, *The Eternal Galilean*, pp. 214, 216.
32. Fulton J. Sheen, *The Priest Is Not His Own* (New York: McGraw-Hill, 1963), p. 191.
33. Sheen, *For God and Country*, p. 7.
34. Sheen, *The Rainbow of Sorrow*, pp. 11–12.
35. Sheen, *Calvary and the Mass*, pp. 25, 68.
36. Sheen, *The Life of All Living*, pp. 98–99.
37. See Sheen, *Those Mysterious Priests*, p. 117.
38. Sheen, *The Rainbow of Sorrow*, p. 14.

CHAPTER FOUR

1. Fulton J. Sheen, *Peace of Soul* (Liguori, Mo.: Triumph, 1949), p. 118.
2. See Sheen, *Treasure in Clay*, pp. 267–268.
3. John Paul II, Apostolic Exhortation on Reconciliation and Penance, *Reconciliatio et Paenitentia*, 32.
4. Sheen, *These Are the Sacraments*, p. 72.
5. Sheen, *Moods and Truths*, p. 39.
6. See Sheen, *Peace of Soul*, pp. 130–131.
7. Sheen, *These Are the Sacraments*, p. 12.
8. Sheen, *These Are the Sacraments*, pp. 72–74.
9. See Sheen, *The Priest Is Not His Own*, p. 99.
10. Sheen, *These Are the Sacraments*, p. 74.
11. Sheen, *Peace of Soul*, p. 131.
12. Sheen, *These Are the Sacraments*, p. 85.
13. John Paul II, *Reconciliatio et Paenitentia*, 31.
14. Sheen, *Moods and Truths*, p. 51.
15. Sheen, *Guide to Contentment*, pp. 168–169.
16. Sheen, *Peace of Soul*, p. 120.
17. Sheen, *For God and Country*, p. 27.
18. Sheen, *These Are the Sacraments*, p. 88.
19. Sheen, *These Are the Sacraments*, p. 72.
20. John Paul II, *Reconciliatio et Paenitentia*, 31.
21. Sheen, *Treasure in Clay*, p. 265. Emphasis in original.
22. Sheen, *The Priest Is Not His Own*, p. 46.
23. Sheen, *Go to Heaven*, p. 156.
24. Sheen, *These Are the Sacraments*, p. 72.
25. John Paul II, *Reconciliatio et Paenitentia*, no. 29.
26. Sheen, *Go to Heaven*, p. 55.
27. Sheen, *These Are the Sacraments*, p. 88.

CHAPTER FIVE

1. Sheen, *The Priest Is Not His Own*, p. 214.
2. Sheen, *Treasure in Clay*, p. 187.
3. Sheen, *Treasure in Clay*, p. 352.
4. See Sheen, *Treasure in Clay*, p. 189.
5. See *Lumen Gentium*, 11 and CCC 1324.
6. *Ecclesia de Eucharistia*, 1.
7. *Presbyterorum Ordinis*, 5; see St. Thomas Aquinas, *Summa Theologiae* III, q. 65, a. 3, ad. 1; q. 79, a. 1, c. and ad. 1.

8. Sheen, *The Mystical Body of Christ*, p. 374.
9. Sheen, *Those Mysterious Priests*, p. 148.
10. Sheen, *The Mystical Body of Christ*, p. 349.
11. Sheen, *Those Mysterious Priests*, p. 148.
12. Sheen, *Calvary and the Mass*, p. 62.
13. Fulton J. Sheen, *Life of Christ* (New York: McGraw-Hill, 1958), pp. 143–144. Emphasis in original.
14. See Sheen, *Those Mysterious Priests*, p. 149.
15. Sheen, *Those Mysterious Priests*, p. 149.
16. Sheen, *The Priest Is Not His Own*, p. 17.
17. Sheen, *The Life of All Living*, p. 102.
18. Sheen, *The Priest Is Not His Own*, p. 204.
19. Sheen, *The Mystical Body of Christ*, p. 5.
20. Sheen, *Go to Heaven*, p. 142.
21. Sheen, *The Mystical Body of Christ*, p. 363.
22. Sheen, *The Mystical Body of Christ*, p. 363.
23. Sheen, *Life of Christ*, p. 140.
24. Sheen, *Those Mysterious Priests*, p. 166.
25. *Sacramentum Caritatis*, 66, quoting Augustine, *Enarrationes in Psalmos* 98:9, CCL XXXIX, 1385.
26. Sheen, *Those Mysterious Priests*, p. 185.
27. Sheen, *The Priest Is Not His Own*, p. 240.
28. Sheen, *Treasure in Clay*, p. 189.
29. Cardinal Joseph Ratzinger, *The Spirit of the Liturgy* (San Francisco: Ignatius, 2000), p. 193.
30. Ratzinger, *The Spirit of the Liturgy*, p. 194.

CHAPTER SIX
1. Sheen, *The Priest Is Not His Own*, p. 85. (Author's translation).
2. Sheen, *Treasure in Clay*, p. 169.
3. See Sheen, *Treasure in Clay*, p. 91.
4. See *Lumen Gentium*, 10.
5. St. Thomas Aquinas, *Summa Theologica*, Supplement q. 37, a. 2, ad. 3.
6. Sheen, *The Mystical Body of Christ*, p. 354.
7. Sheen, *The Priest Is Not His Own*, p. 226.
8. *Presbyterorum Ordinis*, 2.
9. *Presbyterorum Ordinis*, 5.
10. *Presbyterorum Ordinis*, 14.
11. *Lumen Gentium*, 28. See also CCC 1566.

12. Pope Benedict XVI, General Audience on Psalm 110, November 16, 2011.

13. Pope Benedict XVI, Homily on the Solemnity of Corpus Christi, June 3, 2010.

14. Sheen, *The Priest Is Not His Own*, pp. 196–197.

15. See John Paul II, Apostolic Letter on the Dignity and Vocation of Women, *Mulieris Dignitatem*, 26–27.

16. John Paul II. Apostolic Letter on Reserving Priestly Ordination to Men Alone, *Ordinatio Sacerdotalis*, 4.

17. Cardinal Joseph Ratzinger, *Responsum ad Propositum Dubium* Concerning the Teaching Contained in *Ordinatio Sacerdotalis*, Congregation for the Doctrine of the Faith, October 28, 1995.

18. Sheen, *The World's First Love*, p. 176.

19. Sheen, *The World's First Love*, p. 177.

20. Sheen, *The Priest Is Not His Own*, p. 269.

21. Sheen, *Those Mysterious Priests*, p. 310.

22. Sheen, *Calvary and the Mass*, p. 109.

23. Sheen, *The Priest Is Not His Own*, p. 17.

24. Sheen, *The Priest Is Not His Own*, p. 77.

25. Sheen, *Those Mysterious Priests*, p. 92.

26. Sheen, *Those Mysterious Priests*, p. 219.

27. Sheen, *Those Mysterious Priests*, p. 103.

28. Sheen, *Those Mysterious Priests*, p. 84.

29. Sheen, *The Priest Is Not His Own*, p. 165.

CHAPTER SEVEN

1. Fulton J. Sheen, *The Divine Romance* (New York: Alba House, 1996), p. 102.

2. Fulton J. Sheen, *Footprints in a Darkened Forest* (New York: Meredith, 1967), p. 249.

3. Sheen, *Those Mysterious Priests*, p. 239.

4. Sheen, *The Mystical Body of Christ*, p. 101, n.1.

5. Sheen, *The Mystical Body of Christ*, p. 101.

6. *Lumen Gentium*, 25.

7. Sheen, *The Mystical Body of Christ*, p. 188.

8. Sheen, *The Mystical Body of Christ*, p. 98.

9. Sheen, *Go to Heaven*, p. 103.

10. See Sheen, *Life of Christ*, p. 107.

11. Although it is routinely said that Saul's name was changed to Paul, the fact is that he went by two names. Being a Roman citizen, "Paul" was his Roman (Gentile) name, while "Saul" was his Jewish name. He was not given a new name by God.

12. Fulton J. Sheen, *Characters of the Passion* (New York: Garden City, 1953), p. 21.

13. Sheen, *Characters of the Passion*, p. 16.

14. Sheen, *The Priest Is Not His Own*, p. 181.

15. Sheen, *The Cross and the Beatitudes*, p. 34.

16. Sheen, *Characters of the Passion*, p. 21.

17. Sheen, *Guide to Contentment*, p. 93.

18. Sheen, *The Priest Is Not His Own*, p. 185.

19. Sheen, *The Priest Is Not His Own*, p. 189.

20. Sheen, *The Mystical Body of Christ*, p. 167. Emphasis in original.

21. Sheen, *The Mystical Body of Christ*, p. 146. Emphasis in original.

22. Sheen, *Those Mysterious Priests*, p. 143.

23. Sheen, *The Mystical Body of Christ*, p. 156.

24. Sheen, *Treasure in Clay*, p. 244.

25. See Fulton J. Sheen, *Whence Come Wars* (New York: Sheed and Ward, 1940), pp. 92–96.

26. Sheen, *The Mystical Body of Christ*, p. 151.

27. Sheen, *Treasure in Clay*, p. 102. Emphasis in original.

CHAPTER EIGHT

1. Sheen, *The World's First Love*, p. 64.

2. Sheen, *Treasure in Clay*, p. 316.

3. See Sheen, *Treasure in Clay*, p. 323.

4. Sheen, *Treasure in Clay*, p. 315.

5. Sheen, *The Mystical Body of Christ*, p. 328.

6. Sheen, *Go to Heaven*, p. 177.

7. Sheen, *Moods and Truths*, p. 100.

8. *Lumen Gentium*, 56.

9. Sheen, *Seven Words of Jesus and Mary*, p. 44.

10. Sheen, *The World's First Love*, pp. 12–13.

11. Sheen, *Moods and Truths*, p. 108.

12. Sheen, *The World's First Love*, p. 15.

13. Sheen, *The World's First Love*, p. 18.

14. Sheen, *The World's First Love*, p. 16.

15. Sheen, *The World's First Love*, p. 169.

16. Sheen, *Calvary and the Mass*, p. 54.

17. Sheen, *The World's First Love*, p. 78.
18. Sheen, *The Way of the Cross*, p. 20.
19. Sheen, *Life of Christ*, p. 21.
20. Sheen, *The Mystical Body of Christ*, p. 322. Emphasis in original.
21. Sheen, *Life of Christ*, p. 36.
22. Sheen, *Calvary and the Mass*, p. 53.
23. Sheen, *The Eternal Galilean*, p. 246.
24. Sheen, *The Divine Romance*, p. 91.
25. Sheen, *The Eternal Galilean*, p. 255.
26. Sheen, *The World's First Love*, p. 265.
27. Sheen, *The Eternal Galilean*, pp. 257–258.
28. Sheen, *Seven Words of Jesus and Mary*, p. 12.
29. Fulton J. Sheen, *The Seven Virtues* (New York: P.J. Kenedy & Sons, 1940), p. 55.
30. Sheen, *The World's First Love*, p. 141.
31. Sheen, *Seven Words of Jesus and Mary*, p. 91.
32. Sheen, *The World's First Love*, p. 123.
33. Sheen, *The World's First Love*, p. 103.
34. Sheen, *Moods and Truths*, p. 101.
35. From "The Virgin," by William Wordsworth, quoted in Sheen, *The World's First Love*, p. 271.
36. Pope John Paul II, *Rosarium Virginis Mariae*, 1.

CHAPTER NINE
1. Sheen, *Old Errors and New Labels*, p. 289.
2. Sheen, *Philosophies at War*, p. 135.
3. Fulton J. Sheen, *Three to Get Married* (New York: Scepter, 1996), p. 148.
4. Sheen, *Life of Christ*, p. 375.
5. Pope Paul VI, Encyclical on the Regulation of Birth, *Humanae Vitae*, 14.
6. Sheen, *Old Errors and New Labels*, p. 294.
7. Sheen, *The World's First Love*, p. 122.
8. Sheen, *Love One Another*, p. 12.
9. Pope John Paul II, *Man and Woman He Created Them: A Theology of the Body*, trans. Michael Waldstein (Boston: Pauline, 2006), p. 633. Emphasis in original.
10. Pope Paul VI, *Humanae Vitae*, 17.
11. Sheen, *Three to Get Married*, pp. 152–153.
12. Sheen, *Three to Get Married*, p. 148.

13. Sheen, *The Moral Universe*, p. 107.
14. Sheen, *The Power of Love*, p. 96; see Mark 10:13–16.
15. Sheen, *The Cross and the Beatitudes*, p. 42.
16. Sheen, *Three to Get Married*, p. 156.
17. See C.S. Lewis, *The Abolition of Man* (New York: HarperCollins, 2001), pp. 9, 11.
18. Pope John Paul II, *Man and Woman He Created Them: A Theology of the Body*, p. 637.
19. See Paul VI, *Humanae Vitae*, 10.
20. Sheen, *Those Mysterious Priests*, p. 142.
21. Reeves, p. 336.
22. Sheen, *Old Errors and New Labels*, p. 298.

CHAPTER TEN
1. Sheen, *The Seven Virtues*, pp. 75–76.
2. Sheen, *Three to Get Married*, p. 204.
3. Sheen, *Philosophies at War*, p. 120.
4. I have left this Greek term untranslated here and later in this chapter when I cite Matthew 5:32 because there is wide disagreement over its precise meaning in English.
5. Sheen, *Three to Get Married*, p. 188.
6. Sheen, *Philosophies at War*, pp. 129–130.
7. Sheen, *The Moral Universe*, p. 84.
8. Sheen, *Three to Get Married*, p. 1.
9. Sheen, *Three to Get Married*, p. 8.
10. Sheen, *The Seven Virtues*, p. 53.
11. Sheen, *Go to Heaven*, p. 134.
12. See Sheen, *Three to Get Married*, p. 191.
13. Sheen, *Three to Get Married*, p. 181.
14. Sheen, *Three to Get Married*, p. 37.
15. Sheen, *Three to Get Married*, pp. 183–184.
16. Sheen, *A Declaration of Dependence*, p. 76.
17. Fulton J. Sheen, *Life Is Worth Living* (New York: McGraw-Hill, 1953), pp. 102–103.
18. Sheen, *Go to Heaven*, pp. 72–73.
19. John Paul II, *Familiaris Consortio*, 33.
20. Sheen, *Life Is Worth Living*, p. 102; see 1 Corinthians 7:14.
21. Pius XI, encyclical, On Christian Marriage, *Casti Connubii*, 37.
22. Sheen, *Three to Get Married*, p. 113.

SELECTED BIBLIOGRAPHY

WORKS BY FULTON J. SHEEN

Calvary and the Mass. New York: Garden City, 1953.

Characters of the Passion. New York: Garden City, 1953.

Children and Parents. New York: Simon and Schuster, 1970.

Communism and the Conscience of the West. Indianapolis: Bobbs-Merrill, 1948.

The Cross and the Beatitudes. New York: Garden City, 1952.

The Cross and the Crisis. Freeport: Books for Libraries, 1969.

Declaration of Dependence, A. Milwaukee: Bruce, 1941.

The Divine Romance. New York: Alba, 1996.

The Eternal Galilean. New York: Garden City, 1950.

Footprints in a Darkened Forest. New York: Meredith, 1967.

For God and Country. New York: P.J. Kenedy & Sons, 1941.

Freedom under God. Milwaukee: Bruce, 1940.

The Fullness of Christ. Huntington, Ind.: Our Sunday Visitor / National Council of Catholic Men, 1935.

Go to Heaven. London: Catholic Book Club, 1962.

God and Intelligence in Modern Philosophy: A Critical Study in the Light of the Philosophy of St. Thomas. New York: Longmans, Green, 1930.

God and War. New York: P.J. Kenedy & Sons, 1942.

God Love You. New York: Garden City, 1955.

Guide to Contentment. New York: Alba, 1996.

Liberty, Equality and Fraternity. New York: Macmillian, 1938.

Life Is Worth Living. New York: McGraw-Hill, 1953.

Life Is Worth Living: Fifth Series. New York: McGraw-Hill, 1957.

Life Is Worth Living: Fourth Series. New York: McGraw-Hill, 1956.

Life Is Worth Living: Second Series. New York: McGraw-Hill, 1954.

The Life of All Living. New York: Popular Library, 1958.

Life of Christ. New York: McGraw-Hill, 1958.

Lift Up Your Heart. New York: McGraw-Hill, 1960.

Love One Another. New York: Garden City, 1953.

Manifestations of Christ. Huntington, Ind.: Our Sunday Visitor / National Council of Catholic Men, 1932.

Missions and the World Crisis. Milwaukee: Bruce, 1963.

Moods and Truths. New York: Garden City, 1950.

The Moral Universe: A Preface to Christian Living. Milwaukee: Bruce, 1936.

The Mystical Body of Christ. New York: Sheed and Ward, 1935.

Old Errors and New Labels. New York: Garden City, 1950.

On Being Human. Garden City: Doubleday, 1982.

Peace of Soul. Liguori, Mo.: Triumph, 1949.

Philosophies at War. New York: Charles Scribner's Sons, 1943.

Philosophy of Religion. New York: Appleton-Century-Crofts, 1948.

Philosophy of Science. Milwaukee: Bruce, 1934.

The Power of Love. New York: Charles Scribner's Sons, 1964.

Preface to Religion. New York: P.J. Kenedy & Sons, 1946.

The Priest Is Not His Own. New York: McGraw-Hill, 1963.

The Rainbow of Sorrow. New York: Garden City, 1953.

Religion without God. New York: Garden City, 1954.

Science, Psychiatry and Religion. New York: Dell, 1962.

Seven Words of Jesus and Mary. New York: Garden City, 1953.

Seven Words to the Cross. New York: P.J. Kenedy & Sons, 1944.

The Seven Capital Sins. New York: Alba, 2001.

The Seven Last Words. New York: Alba, 1996.

The Seven Pillars of Peace. New York: Charles Scribner's Sons, 1944.

The Seven Virtues. New York: P.J. Kenedy & Sons, 1940.

These Are the Sacraments. New York: Hawthorn, 1962.

Thinking Life Through. New York: McGraw-Hill, 1955.

This Is Rome. New York: Hawthorn, 1960.

The Way of the Cross. Huntington, Ind.: Our Sunday Visitor, 1982.

The World's First Love. San Francisco: Ignatius, 1996.

PAPAL WRITINGS

Benedict XVI. Apostolic Exhortation on the Eucharist as the Source and Summit of the Church's Life and Mission, *Sacramentum Caritatis.*

———. General Audience on Psalm 110, November 16, 2011.

———. Homily on the Solemnity of Corpus Christi, June 3, 2010.

John Paul II. *Man and Woman He Created Them: A Theology of the Body.* Translated by Michael Waldstein. Boston: Pauline, 2006.

———. Apostolic Letter on the Christian Meaning of Human Suffering, *Salvifici Doloris.*

———. Encyclical on the Eucharist and Its Relationship to the Church, *Ecclesia de Eucharistia.*

———. Apostolic Letter on Reserving Priestly Ordination to Men Alone, *Ordinatio Sacerdotalis.*

———. Apostolic Letter on the Rosary of the Virgin Mary, *Rosarium Virginis Mariae.*

———. Apostolic Exhortation on the Role of the Christian Family in the Modern World, *Familiaris Consortio.*

———. Apostolic Exhortation on Reconciliation and Penance, *Reconciliatio et Paenitentia.*

Paul VI. Encyclical on the Regulation of Birth, *Humanae Vitae*.

Pius XI. Encyclical on Christian Marriage, *Casti Connubii*.

OTHER RESOURCES

Catechism of the Catholic Church, Second Edition. Washington, D.C.: United States Catholic Conference—Libreria Editrice Vaticana, 1997.

Decree on the Ministry and Life of Priests, *Presbyterorum Ordinis*.

The Dogmatic Constitution on the Church, *Lumen Gentium*.

The Pastoral Constitution on the Church in the Modern World, *Gaudium et Spes*.

Ratzinger, Joseph. "Responsum ad Propositum Dubium Concerning the Teaching Contained in *Ordinatio Sacerdotalis*," Congregation for the Doctrine of the Faith. October 28, 1995.

Ratzinger, Joseph. *The Spirit of the Liturgy*. San Francisco: Ignatius, 2000.

Reeves, Thomas C. *America's Bishop: The Life and Times of Fulton J. Sheen*. New York: Encounter, 2001.

Rodriguez, Janel. *Meet Fulton Sheen: Beloved Preacher and Teacher of the Word*. Cincinnati: Servant, 2006.

Thomas Aquinas. *Summa Theologica*, Translated by Fathers of the English Dominican Province. 5 vols. New York: Benziger Brothers, 1948.

ABOUT THE AUTHOR

Mark J. Zia, s.t.d., is associate professor of theology and director of academic enrichment programs at Benedictine College in Atchison, Kansas, where he has worked for the past ten years. He travels around the country instructing candidates for ordination to the permanent diaconate. Zia has a doctorate in dogmatic theology from the Pontifical University of the Holy Cross in Rome, and an undergraduate degree from the Franciscan University of Steubenville, Ohio. He is married and the father of seven children.